W9-BLN-986

The Andrews FAMILY

BASEBALL'S GREAT MOMENTS

Action-packed accounts of the most memora-
ble performances in baseball history. Herb
Gluck recreates Sandy Koufax's perfect game,
Hank Aaron's 715th home run, Joe DiMaggio's
56-game hitting streak, and nine other major
league highlights.

MAJOR LEAGUE
LIBRARY

illustrated with photographs

BASEBALL'S
GREAT MOMENTS

BY HERB GLUCK

Random House · New York

COPYRIGHT © 1975 by Random House, Inc.
All rights reserved under International and Pan-American Copyright Conventions. Published in the United States by Random House, Inc., New York, and simultaneously in Canada by Random House of Canada Limited, Toronto.

LIBRARY OF CONGRESS CATALOGING IN PUBLICATION DATA
Gluck, Herb. Baseball's great moments. (Major league library)
SUMMARY: Presents major league baseball highlights from the early 1900's to the present.
1. Baseball—Biography—Juvenile literature. 2. Baseball—History—Juvenile literature.
[1. Baseball—biography. 2. Baseball—History] I. Title.
GV865.A1G58   796.357'092'2 [B]   74–23539
ISBN 0–394–83030–X   ISBN 0–394–93030–4 (lib. bdg.)
Manufactured in the United States of America   1 2 3 4 5 6 7 8 9 0

PHOTOGRAPH CREDITS: Culver Pictures, Inc., 127; Ken Regan (Camera 5), 93, 124; United Press International, endpapers, 4–5, 7, 15, 22, 26–27, 45, 51, 53, 59, 66, 75, 78, 96, 99, 105, 110, 112, 115, 116, 133, 140, 144; Wide World Photos, 2, 17, 31 left and right, 37, 41, 54, 72, 83, 85, 89, 122, 131, 137.

Cover photograph by Ken Regan (Camera 5).

To **ABBEY,** who is the greatest.

CONTENTS

INTRODUCTION

Major league baseball is a sport that deals in superlatives. During the course of a season, hardly a day goes by without the mention of the *greatest* pitching performance, the *most exciting* fielding play, the *longest* home run. Baseball buffs enjoy few things more than swapping stories about the game's magic moments. It all began in 1869, when the Cincinnati Red Stockings suited up as baseball's first professional team. And today, in an era of wide expansion, of innovation and change, the sport seems to capture our imagination more than ever.

When we think of great moments, it is usually the individual triumphs that first come to mind. Hank Aaron hammering out his 715th home run in 1974; Cookie Lavagetto slamming a ninth-inning double to break up a World Series no-hitter in 1947; Carl Hubbell striking out Babe Ruth, Lou Gehrig, Jimmy

Foxx, Al Simmons, and Joe Cronin in the 1934 All-Star game; and Sandy Koufax pitching a perfect game in 1965 are just four examples of the major leaguer at his very best. Superstars like Joe DiMaggio, Ted Williams, and Willie Mays had so many great moments during their outstanding careers that it was difficult to choose a single achievement to highlight, but their stories are here, too.

Then there is the very special kind of greatness that is achieved not by one man but by nine. Pooling their talents in an incredible team effort, the Philadelphia A's pulled off an amazing come-from-behind rally on their way to the 1929 world championship.

Baseball's Great Moments recaptures the excitement of all these moments and many more. We've even included one of the greatest blunders in baseball history—Fred Merkle's "bonehead play" during the 1908 race.

Of course there are enough dramatic moments in baseball to fill an encyclopedia. The twelve stories that follow are just a sampling of the countless remarkable contests involving the great players of the past and present, and there are sure to be dozens more in the years to come. Every reader will have his own favorites. Hopefully, we've included some of yours— and some that may be brand new to you.

HENRY AARON

The Hammer's Biggest Homer

On April 8, 1974, the pre-game show at Atlanta Stadium glittered in bursts of color. The vast assembly of 53,775 fans rose to their feet as Henry Aaron walked out on the field through lines of majorettes. Hundreds of balloons floated in the night air, the electronic scoreboard flashed HANK, and brightly painted banners fluttered from the stands proclaiming: MOVE OVER BABE . . . BAD HENRY WILL DO IT . . . THE HAMMER WILL NAIL IT TONIGHT . . . and simply NO. 715!

A huge map of the United States, painted in red, white, and blue stars and stripes, covered a wide patch of the outfield grass. The many friends and relatives of Henry Aaron were gathered near home plate. Motion picture stars shook the Atlanta slugger's hand, and Pearl Bailey, backed by the Jonesboro High School

11

band and the Morris Brown College choir, sang the national anthem. After the last strains were drowned out by a roar of anticipation, the Braves poured out of the dugout. But every eye in the packed stands was trained on one man—Hammerin' Henry Aaron.

A few days earlier, Aaron had hammered out his 714th homer, tying the legendary Babe Ruth in career home run production. And now, Henry was hoping to go ahead. The Babe had hit number 714 in 1935, and for more than 30 years, that standard had seemed way beyond the means of ordinary mortals. In 1935 no other player had hit even as many as 400 homers (Lou Gehrig, the Babe's nearest competitor, had only 350). It seemed impossible to imagine any other slugger ever approaching Ruth's mark. But then, four decades later, along came Henry Louis Aaron.

The road to number 715 had been a long and hard one. After joining the Braves in 1954, Aaron got off to a good, but not great, start. The 20-year-old outfielder finished his rookie season with 27 doubles, 6 triples, and 13 home runs for a .280 average. The next season his totals jumped to 37 doubles (best in the league), 9 triples, and 27 home runs. In the years that followed, Hank's batting average was rarely below .300.

He continued to knock out home runs at a steady rate which never went below 24 or above 44. He hammered out his 100th four-bagger in 1957, his 200th in 1960, and by 1966 he had passed the 400 mark. His consistent contributions soon put him in the top ranks of baseball, but for years he was one of the game's least publicized heroes. A shy and modest man, he was overshadowed by more flamboyant sluggers like Willie Mays and Mickey Mantle.

But year after year, Aaron was quietly closing in on the most famous record of them all. Home run number 500 came in 1968, and in 1971 he reached 600. Then on July 21, 1973, Aaron belted out his 700th home run and found himself smack in the middle of the lime-light. By that time it was clear that Henry Aaron was well on his way to breaking Babe Ruth's home run mark—the one baseball record that fans and experts had always considered unreachable. For the rest of the '73 season, the Atlanta clubhouse was flooded with telegrams and letters, most of them wishing Aaron well in his quest for the all-time record.

However, there were also wild and vicious messages denouncing him for his efforts. Some were the ravings of baseball fanatics who simply couldn't bear the thought of an "upstart" like Aaron daring to challenge the immortal Babe; others were from sick-minded bigots who anonymously threatened the black super-star's life. Through it all, Aaron maintained his composure.

"I have a job to do," he said calmly. "When the final curtain comes down, my career will speak for itself."

As the '73 season drew to an end, the countdown began. Aaron picked up numbers 710, 711, 712. Then on September 29, 1973, he stepped into a pitch thrown by Jerry Reuss of the Houston Astros. The ball landed in the center-field stands of Atlanta Stadium, a huge number 713 went up on the electronic scoreboard, and Henry Aaron advanced to within one swing of Babe Ruth's "unreachable" record.

The next day, September 30, was the last game of the season, and baseball fans all over the world were watching to see if Hank could hit his 714th homer before the season ended. Some 40,000 Braves fans packed Atlanta Stadium to watch the 1973 finale unfold.

Aaron wanted a home run that day more than anything in the world. But all he could manage in his first three at-bats were three singles. On any other day he would have been more than pleased with that kind of performance; but this wasn't just any day. It was Aaron's last chance that season to tie Ruth's record, and nothing but a home run would do.

In the eighth inning Henry whipped his bat around on an inside fastball and popped it weakly into the air for an infield out. For Henry Aaron, the game—and the season—were over. He would have a long winter of waiting before he got another chance to go after the elusive number 714—and the magic 715!

As disappointed as he was, Aaron knew that it was only a matter of time before he reached his goal. "All I've got to do to get the record," he said, "is to stay alive."

The winter months came and went while Henry waited. Basketball, hockey, and football dominated the sports scene. Then, three months before the '74

After hammering out his 713th home run on September 28, 1973, Hank Aaron gives his fans a clenched fist salute.

baseball season started, the Magnavox Corporation held a press conference in New York City. Magnavox had just signed Aaron to a long-term contract that would make the Atlanta slugger an instant millionaire. It would be Henry's job to act as a spokesman for a variety of the company's products.

Magnavox immediately began a massive national publicity campaign in order to get the most mileage out of their famous new representative. In the midst of the big build-up, Brave manager Eddie Mathews and board chairman Bill Bartholomay announced that they would keep Henry out of the line-up for the entire opening series—which was scheduled to take place in Cincinnati—so that he could hit *the* home run at home.

That statement set off a controversy that rocked the major leagues. Baseball commissioner Bowie Kuhn declared that he expected Aaron to appear in the opening series. He said that every team was obligated to put its best players on the field at all times—and no one could deny that Aaron was one of the best Braves. The commissioner then added that any violation of his order would be regarded as an affront to the game itself.

Henry Aaron was caught in the middle of the dispute. "I would like number 714 and number 715 to be hit in Atlanta," he admitted. Henry had been playing there ever since the Braves had moved from Milwaukee to Atlanta eight years earlier. All his friends and family were there. Naturally, he wanted his big moment to occur at home.

Mathews and Bartholomay reluctantly agreed to Kuhn's demand. When the 1974 season opened in Cincinnati on April 4, Henry was in the line-up. And in the first inning of that first game, on his first swing of the bat, Hammerin' Henry Aaron hit the 714th home run of his career off Red pitcher Jack Billingham. As the ball dropped over the fence in left center, Red outfielder Pete Rose helplessly watched its flight and 52,154 Cincinnati fans rose from their seats to salute the rival slugger.

On April 4, 1974, Aaron takes a historic swing for home run number 714, the one that tied Babe Ruth's all-time record.

Henry barely had time to celebrate his incredible achievement before he was again involved in the bitter dispute. For that night, manager Mathews announced he would bench his star for the remaining two games of the Cincinnati series.

Kuhn would have none of it. Right after the second game in Cincinnati—a game in which Aaron didn't play—the commissioner issued a strong statement to the Atlanta management. "Aaron *must* play tomorrow," said Kuhn. "This is a direct order, and I haven't decided the consequences [if he doesn't], but they will be severe."

Aaron was in the line-up for the last game of the series in Cincinnati on Sunday, April 7. In three times at bat, he struck out twice and grounded out once. The next game was a Monday night contest against the Los Angeles Dodgers—in Atlanta.

That night the overflow crowd in Atlanta Stadium stirred nervously in their seats. Tension could be felt in the stands, the dugouts, up in the press box, and out on the playing field. Millions of fans across the nation tuned in to the Monday night telecast to see Aaron make his bid for home run number 715.

On the mound for the Dodgers was little Al Downing, who didn't seem at all worried about his role in Aaron's drama. "I won't be pitching any differently tonight," he said coolly during the pre-game ceremony. "I'll mix my pitches up, and if I make a mistake . . . it's no disgrace."

Downing didn't make any mistakes the first time he

faced Aaron that night. He worked his pitches so carefully that Hank never even took the bat off his shoulder. Leading off the bottom of the second inning, the Atlanta star took a ball, a called strike, then watched three wide serves breeze past him. Tossing his bat aside, Aaron took first base on a walk.

The hometown spectators jeered and booed the Dodger southpaw as if he had committed an unpardonable sin. They kept up the clamor until Dusty Baker sent Aaron home on a double. Only then did the jeers turn to cheers. By crossing the plate, Aaron had just broken the National League scoring record of 2,063 runs held by Willie Mays.

But the roar seemed like a whisper in comparison to the din that followed in the fourth inning. The Dodgers had grabbed a 3–1 lead in the third inning, and now it was the bottom of the fourth. As third baseman Darrell Evans came to the plate, Henry Aaron walked to the on-deck circle. All eyes were on Henry as Evans made it safely to first on a mishandled grounder.

Then the stadium really shook as Hammerin' Henry stepped into the batter's box for his second at-bat. Nothing—not even the light drizzle that descended on the thousands of umbrellas raised in the stands—could detract from the excitement.

Al Downing peered in for a sign, glanced over at first, then threw a fastball low and inside: Ball one.

Then came the second pitch, another fastball right down the upper middle of the plate. Aaron unleashed his first cut of the night. With a flick of his wrists, he sent the ball sailing through the drizzle and toward the 385-foot sign in left-center field. Dodger outfielders Bill Buckner and Jimmy Wynn drifted back toward the fence. Buckner was closest to the plummeting ball. Bracing himself, he started to climb the fence but gave up as the ball dropped over the 6-foot wall that separated the bull pen from the outfield.

There was a momentary stillness, as if a vacuum had been created to shut out the sound and fury of the blow. Then, the noise freed itself in a gigantic roar!

But the initial moment of hysteria had not yet caught up with Aaron. In a rare departure from his normal habit of not following the flight of a long drive off his bat, he seemed as intent as anyone else in watching his home run disappear behind the fence. Then, moving easily around the basepaths, he flashed a big grin. It was over. Henry Aaron had just hit one more homer than any other man in history.

Atlanta reliever Tom House triumphantly emerged from the bull pen with the home run ball. It was buried in the webbing of his glove. Entertainer Sammy Davis had placed a $25,000 price tag on the record-breaking ball before the start of the game, but House held his treasure aloft as if it was worth a million.

By the time House reached the plate, Aaron was up on the shoulders of his teammates, who were gleefully milling around the field. Henry's parents joined the celebration and proudly hugged their smiling son.

As the happy swarm of players, officials, and fans

tried to touch Aaron, to pound his broad back in a show of affection, Henry moved over to the field box where his wife Billye was seated. The 53,000 spectators cheered as the Aarons embraced.

This was no time for baseball. Fireworks shot up into the Atlanta sky, the scoreboard flashed in pulsating brilliance: 715! . . . 715! . . . 715!

At 9:08 p.m., on April 8, 1974, there was a pause for history! Tom House threaded his way to the field box seats and jammed *the* ball into Henry Aaron's hand. Then Bill Bartholomay stepped to a microphone and presented Aaron with a diamond-encrusted ring bearing replicas of the Atlanta slugger and Atlanta Stadium.

Monte Irvin, representing Bowie Kuhn, handed Aaron a solid-gold wristwatch. But when Irvin mentioned the commissioner's name, the crowd sent up a chorus of boos. The controversy of the past few days in Cincinnati had not endeared Kuhn to the Atlanta fans, and now they wanted the commissioner to know how they felt. As Irvin valiantly tried to make his voice heard above the racket, Aaron grinned happily.

The pandemonium lasted a full eleven minutes. Then, the game continued. The Dodgers scored a run in the sixth inning, and the Braves came back with two in their half of the frame. The game finally ended with the Braves on top.

Champagne flowed in the Braves' clubhouse before the newsmen were admitted for post-game interviews. When the door finally opened, the reporters rushed into the locker room to get the biggest story of their baseball lives.

But Henry Aaron had something important to say before the questions could be fired at him. He had lived under a cloud of suspicion ever since the start of

Aaron is congratulated by teammate Tom House, the man who retrieved the ball after Hank's 715th homer on April 8, 1974.

the season when it was rumored that he was saving number 715 for Atlanta. Now he wanted to set things straight.

"I've read stories that I wasn't trying in my last game in Cincinnati," he began. "I'd just like to say that I have never stepped on a field without doing my level best. I'm not directing this at anyone in particular, but when it is said that you're a disgrace on the field, something has to be said."

Then he turned to a happier subject—his most important hit ever. "It wasn't one of my better ones," he said of his record shot off Downing. "I hit it fairly good, though, and the wind helped carry it. I was guessing. Downing threw me fastballs the first time up, and I thought he'd start me that way the next time and then go to breaking balls. But he threw the fastball again. He got it up a little bit, and I was fortunate enough to hit it."

Aaron was bombarded with questions by the eager reporters in the jam-packed room. "Do you consider yourself the best hitter who ever played the game?" asked one of the newsmen.

"Now I can consider myself one of the best," he answered. "Maybe not *the* best because a lot of great ones have played this game—DiMaggio, Mays, Jackie Robinson—those three, in that order. But I think I can fit in there somehow.

"I wouldn't say Henry Aaron is going to be fourth," he added with a grin. "I'd say Henry Aaron is going to be second or third."

The cheering had long stopped by the time the weary home run king finally got to sleep at about 6 a.m. He got up early that afternoon and went right over to the Braves office. A huge stack of telegrams was waiting on his secretary's desk. Aaron shook hands with everyone on the administrative staff, then drove to the ball park late in the day, where he sat out the Braves' 9–2 loss to the Dodgers.

Some 24 hours after his historic moment, a bleary-eyed Henry Aaron summed up the last season of his 21-year chase of a legend. "The average person doesn't realize what a nightmare this has been," said Aaron, his energy and emotion drained almost beyond words. "History was set and that's the end of it. Now maybe we can get on with the business of playing baseball again."

THE PHILADELPHIA A's

The Great World Series Rally

The 1929 World Series promised to be a thriller. All season long, the Philadelphia Athletics had dominated the American League. Under the command of veteran manager Connie Mack, the A's had swept to the pennant with 104 wins—18 full games ahead of the second-place Yankees. They had done it with the awesome hitting of Mickey Cochrane, Bing Miller, Mule Haas, Al Simmons, and Jimmy Foxx—and the pitching mastery of George Earnshaw, Lefty Grove, Rube Walberg, Eddie Rommell, and Howard Ehmke. Altogether, the team seemed nearly unbeatable.

But the 1929 National League pennant winners were no slouches themselves. The Chicago Cubs boasted a line-up of super-sluggers like Rogers Hornsby, Kiki Cuyler, Woody English, Hack Wilson,

25

and Riggs Stephenson. And when it came to pitching, they had men like Pat Malone, Charlie Root, Guy Bush, and Sherriff Blake, who could more than hold their own against any mound staff in the majors.

The two teams were so well matched that most fans and experts expected the Series to go the full seven games. In the opener, Cub hurlers Charlie Root and Guy Bush set a combined strikeout record of 13, but

the big Philadelphia bats hammered home a 3–1 victory for the A's. The following day the A's picked up an easy 9–3 win, and it began to look as if the Cubs had been overrated.

But the Cubs bounced back in game three, winning their first Series contest, 3–1, in Philadelphia. And the next day, before 29,991 fans who turned out for game four, Chicago seemed certain to tie up the Series. The

On opening day of the 1929 Series, the crowd at Chicago's Wrigley Field had little to cheer about as the A's downed the Cubs, 3–1.

Cubs went on a hitting spree that put them ahead 8–0 after six-and-a-half innings of play. Throughout those six innings, Cub pitcher Charlie Root, a 19-game winner during the regular season, handcuffed the powerful Philadelphia batters, giving up just three hits.

With the game all but lost, the discouraged Philadelphia fans began to leave the stadium. Al Simmons led off for the A's in the bottom of the seventh before the dwindling crowd. A strong but unorthodox hitter, Simmons tended to step away from the pitch toward third base as he swung. That unusual style never stopped him from tearing the cover off the ball, however. During the regular season he had hit .365, with 34 home runs and 157 runs batted in.

Now Simmons stepped away from a Root pitch and slammed the ball onto the roof of the left-field stands for a home run. The fans perked up somewhat. Chicago 8, Philadelphia 1: At least the A's wouldn't be shut out. Next up was Jimmy Foxx. The Athletics' brawny first baseman had arms as thick as a blacksmith's. Called Double X by his adoring fans, Foxx had hit 33 homers during the season. He had hit a home run in each of the first two Series games, contributing greatly to the two Philadelphia victories. Now, however, he was satisfied to touch Root for a single to right field.

To the plate came Philadelphia right fielder Bing Miller. His season's average was .335, and he had 93 RBI's to his credit. Now he took his stance in the batter's box, picked out a good pitch, and drove the ball up the middle for a base hit. That gave the A's two men on base with no outs. Root appeared to be tiring fast. Cub manager Joe McCarthy got his relief crew up and throwing in the bull pen, but he wasn't worried. After all, his team still led 8–1.

Jimmy Dykes, Philadelphia's hustling little third baseman, came up next and promptly sent Foxx home with a single to left. Shortstop Joe Boley, a .251 hitter who batted eighth in the line-up, then brought Miller home with a single to center. The Cubs' lead had been cut to 8–3.

The fans were now cheering the A's on with every pitch, and the Cubs were beginning to get a little nervous. Everyone in the park sensed that a big rally had gotten underway, but Chicago still had a comfortable five-run lead.

The Cubs relaxed a bit more when Philadelphia pinch-hitter George Burns, batting for pitcher Eddie Rommell, popped up to shortstop Woody English. With his first out of the inning finally under his belt, Root was determined to set the rest of the A's down without further trouble. But Philadelphia's leadoff batter was up next. Max Bishop, a scrawny second baseman who had a fantastic knack for waiting out walks, drilled a Root pitch into center field for a single—and an RBI. Dykes came home, cutting the Cubs lead in half, 8–4.

Chicago manager Joe McCarthy had seen enough. Root had obviously lost his stuff and would have to be replaced. McCarthy marched to the mound, relieved

Root of the ball, and waved in reliever Art Nehf. The 36-year-old lefty was at the tag end of a great career, but McCarthy felt he had enough left to put down the Athletics' rally.

With Boley and Bishop on base and still only one out, Philadelphia's center fielder Mule Haas stepped in to face Nehf. A left-handed batter with a season's average of .313, Haas carefully looked over the old relief pitcher's serves. When he finally found one to his liking, he swung from the toes. The scene that followed was hard to believe. The ball sailed over second base, and center fielder Hack Wilson settled under it for an apparent second out—only to lose sight of the ball in the sun.

At first, Wilson charged toward the ball, thinking it was a sinking liner. But then he realized, to his horror, that it was sailing over his head. He started to run back, but it was too late. The ball rolled into the farthest corner of center field, then skidded to a stop. By the time Wilson caught up with it, Boley and Bishop had run home with Philadelphia's fifth and sixth runs of the inning. And by the time the ball was fired back in, Haas had crossed home plate with an inside-the-park home run.

The fans were up on their feet screaming—with good reason. On that one heart-stopping play, the Athletics had narrowed the score to 8–7. The Cubs still had a one-run lead, but the way the A's were playing, one run hardly seemed like enough.

Nehf was completely unnerved by the calamity out

Two of Philadelphia's biggest bats belonged to Bing Miller (left) and Jimmy Foxx (right), heroes of the run-filled fourth game.

in center field. The crafty southpaw couldn't get the ball over the plate when he faced catcher Mickey Cochrane. The Philadelphia backstop tossed his bat aside and trotted down to first base on a walk.

Manager McCarthy came out to the mound to

make the second pitching change of the inning. With right-handed batters Simmons and Foxx coming up, the Cub manager lifted Nehf and brought in Sherriff Blake. A 29-year-old righty, Blake had won 14 games during the regular season.

But nothing could stop the A's. At bat for the second time in the inning, Simmons singled past the outstretched glove of third baseman Norm McMillan. Then Foxx hit a single up the middle and Cochrane streaked across the plate with the tying run!

The fans had seemed half asleep when the inning started, but now they cheered deliriously while the Athletic players jumped up and down in sheer ecstasy. One player, beside himself with joy, sent Connie Mack, the painfully thin, 67-year-old head of the A's, sprawling to the ground with a hearty slap on his back. Helped to his feet by the embarrassed player, the dignified manager just smiled. "That's all right, son," he said. "*Anything* is all right now!"

As far as Joe McCarthy was concerned, however, nothing was right. The Cub manager yanked Blake out of the game and brought in big Pat Malone from the bull pen. Malone, a barrel-chested 6-foot-2 right-hander, had led the Chicago pitching staff with 22 victories during the regular season. He was scheduled to start the fifth game of the Series; but at this point, McCarthy couldn't have cared less about his pitching rotation. He had to stop the A's now—he would worry about the next day's pitcher later.

Malone's first pitch smacked batter Bing Miller on

his rib cage, and the right fielder trotted to first. The bases were now loaded, and the A's still had only one man out. The next batter, Jimmy Dykes, stepped to the plate and swatted a Malone pitch into the left-field corner for a double. Simmons and Foxx breezed home—and the A's jumped in front of the Cubs, 10–8. Malone finally fanned Boley and Burns to end the long seventh inning. But it was a case of too little, too late. The A's were well on the way to their third big win.

Lefty Grove maintained Philadelphia's hard-won lead by setting down six Cubs in a row in the last two innings. The amazing Philadelphia victory went to Eddie Rommell, who had pitched in the seventh inning, and the Cub loss went to Sherriff Blake.

For overcoming nearly impossible odds, the Athletics' ten-run rally must be viewed as the greatest comeback in World Series history. Their stupendous fourth-game heroics completely demoralized the Cub machine. Two days later, the fifth game was played and another rally in the bottom of the ninth gave the Athletics a 3–2 victory. And with that win, the Philadelphia Athletics wrapped up the 1929 world championship.

GABBY **H**ARTNETT

A Home Run in the Dark

In 1938 Chicago Cub catcher Gabby Hartnett was nearing the end of his great playing career. At one time, his strong throwing arm and skill in handling pitchers had made him the best backstop in the National League, and his clutch hitting had added muscle to the middle of the Chicago batting order. But now Gabby Hartnett was 37 years old—and he had more than just catching and hitting to worry about.

The Cubs had been a National League power since 1929, winning three pennants and finishing second in the league three other times. But now, in the middle of the '38 season, they were barely hanging on to third place.

In an attempt to halt the slide, Cub owner W. K. Wrigley had taken drastic action early in July. He had fired his manager, Charlie Grimm, naming Gabby Hartnett Chicago's new player-manager. Wrigley had been impressed with Hartnett ever since he first saw him as a 21-year-old rookie. He was convinced that his veteran catcher could rally the Cubs and drive them to a pennant victory. After 17 years of big league play, Hartnett was ready for the challenge.

Born in Woonsocket, Rhode Island, on December 20, 1900, Charles Leo Hartnett was brought up to the Cubs in 1922. His genuine enthusiasm and constant chatter behind the plate soon earned him the nickname of Gabby. Later, his teammates dubbed him Old Tomato Face—a fairly accurate description of his weather-reddened complexion.

Hartnett was a big man—6-foot-1 and 195 pounds of muscular power. He had batted over .300 five times since joining the Cubs and was a perennial member of the All-Star team.

But managing a team was a whole different story, as Gabby found out in 1938. For a while he had some trouble adjusting to his new role, and under his uncertain leadership the Cubs continued to stumble around in third place. In fact, by late August they were a full nine games behind the first-place Pirates.

Then, everything began to jell. Slowly but surely, the Cubs began performing at peak level. Depression gave way to determination; sloppy play turned into inspired baseball. Suddenly, in the first weeks of September, the Cubs put together a seven-game winning streak that put them within three-and-a-half games of the Pirates, who just as suddenly had begun to slump.

Two weeks before the end of the season, Chicago played a doubleheader in Brooklyn. The Cubs lost the first game 4–3, but they were leading by two runs after five-and-a-half innings of the second game. In the bottom of the fifth, Dodger outfielder Fred Sington came up. In a driving rain, Sington blasted a home run with a man on base to tie the score.

Play was stopped while the rain continued. Eventually, the umpires called the game. With nothing but a loss and a tie to show for their efforts, the Cubs were still three-and-a-half games behind Pittsburgh.

Hartnett led his team into Philadelphia for a three-game series, but the weather there was just as miserable as it had been in Brooklyn. For three days it rained—and for three days the Cubs did nothing but listen to the radio to find out what was going on in Brooklyn, where the Pirates were scheduled to play the Dodgers. It was raining there, too.

On the fourth day the skies cleared and Chicago and Philadelphia managed to get in a doubleheader. The Cubs took both ends of the twin bill, 4–0 and 2–1. In the first contest Chicago pitcher Bill Lee won his 20th game of the season—gaining his fourth straight shutout. But Pittsburgh beat Brooklyn twice on the same day, so the Cubs gained no ground.

Another Chicago–Philadelphia doubleheader was played the following day, and again the Cubs won both. That same day, however, the Pirates lost to

Chicago got off to a depressingly slow start in 1938. But by late September, Cub player-manager Gabby Hartnett was all smiles.

Cincinnati, leaving the Cubs just two games behind.

The next Chicago series was against the St. Louis Cardinals—at Wrigley Field in Chicago. By then it seemed that Hartnett and his Cubs could do no wrong. They tore into the Cardinals and trounced them by a score of 9–3. Still, the Pirates clung to their two-game margin by also winning a *must* game.

The next day, the two contenders kept pace with each other; they both won. The following Monday, the start of the last week of the season, Pittsburgh had the day off and Chicago played the final game of their series against St. Louis. Chicago won it 6–3 behind Big Bill Lee, cutting the Pittsburgh lead to a game and a half.

Then on Tuesday, September 27, the Pirates and Cubs squared off against each other for the start of their own three-game series. It had come down to a winner-take-all fight to the finish. Now each win—or loss—would count a full game in the standings. The National League pennant winner would almost surely be decided in this series.

With so much riding on each game, Old Tomato Face stuck his neck out and picked Dizzy Dean as his starting pitcher for the series opener. A former Cardinal ace, Dizzy had once been one of the fastest pitchers in baseball. But he had hurt his arm in 1937, and the Cards had traded him to Chicago for a bundle of cash.

The change of climate hadn't seemed to improve Dean's once-powerful arm. He hadn't pitched since September 13 and hadn't started a game since August 20. Nevertheless, Hartnett decided to gamble on Dizzy's heart and his ability to throw under extreme pressure.

Dizzy didn't disappoint Hartnett—or the 42,223 fans who filled Wrigley Field that Tuesday. Despite his aching arm, Dean's control was excellent, while his slow-breaking curves and tired fastballs were almost impossible to hit. Inning after inning, he set the Pirates down, but finally he began to tire. With the Cubs leading 2–0 in the top of the ninth, Pittsburgh third baseman Jeep Hendley crashed a double off the left-center wall, sending runner Woody Jensen to third with two men out.

Hartnett walked to the mound to discuss the critical situation with his exhausted pitcher. "How do you feel?" he asked.

"I reckon you'd better get Big Bill in here," said Dean. "Ol' Diz has gone as far as he can go."

Dean walked off the mound to tremendous applause, and ace starter Bill Lee marched in from the bull pen to pitch to Pittsburg's Al Todd. The first pitch was a strike. Then Todd fouled off a Lee fastball. On the next pitch, Lee uncorked a wild curve that almost made Chicago hearts stop. While Hartnett scrambled for the ball, Jensen scored and Hendley cruised into third base with the tying run.

Lee took a deep breath, pawed at the rubber with his spikes, then pitched a third strike to Todd to end the game. Chicago's 2–1 victory put the team just one-half game out of first place!

Gabby Hartnett was ecstatic over the performance of his Cubs that day, but the best was still to come the following day: September 28, 1938. For the second game of the crucial series Hartnett called on right-handed pitcher Clay Bryant, while Pittsburgh manager Pie Traynor counted on righty Bob Klinger to stop the Cubs.

Hartnett's men grabbed an early lead, stringing a hit and two Pittsburg errors together for a run in the bottom of the second inning. Klinger held Chicago scoreless for the next three innings, but Bryant's crafty pitching protected the Cubs' slim lead.

In the top of the sixth, just as the Chicago fans were beginning to taste victory, the Pirates exploded with three runs. Two walks and three hits, including a home run by Johnny Rizzo, sent Bryant to the showers and put the Pirates on top by the score of 3–1.

In the bottom of the sixth, Hartnett ripped a Klinger pitch for a double, and veteran first baseman Ripper Collins drove Gabby home with another two-bagger. After moving over to third, Collins crossed the plate on a fine bunt by shortstop Billy Jurges to tie up the game, 3–3.

In the seventh inning Vance Page, a 34-year-old relief pitcher, took over for the Cubs and put the Pirates down easily, but Chicago couldn't do anything against Klinger, either.

Hard-hitting Pirate shortstop Arky Vaughan led off the eighth with a walk, then advanced to third on a clean single by Gus Suhr. At that point, manager Hartnett came out of his crouch behind the plate, walked to the mound, and waved right-hander Larry French in from the bull pen.

Pirate manager Pie Traynor countered Hartnett's move with strategy of his own. He sent left-handed swinger Heinie Manush to the plate to pinch-hit for righty Pep Young. Manush, once an All-Star Ameri-

Hartnett was well known as a fine catcher and an excellent manager, but he gained his greatest triumph with his bat.

can League outfielder, came through with a single that
scored Vaughan and gave the lead back to Pittsburgh.

Once again, Hartnett stuck his catcher's mitt under
his arm and trudged out to the mound. For the second
time in two days the Cub manager called Bill Lee in
from the bull pen. The 6-foot-3 ace took his warm-up
tosses, then toed the rubber to face Jeep Hendley with
men on first and second. Lee fired one in, and Hendley
knocked out a long single to drive in the second run of
the inning and put the Pirates ahead 5–3. Then Lee
settled down and got three quick outs without any
further damage.

In the bottom of the eighth, Cub Ripper Collins got
a lead-off single against the tiring Klinger. Pie Traynor then removed his starter and brought in reliever
Bill Swift to prevent a Cub rally. But Swift made
matters worse by walking Billy Jurges. That gave
Chicago the tying runs on base with nobody out. With
pitcher Bill Lee due to bat next, Hartnett went to his
bench for a pinch-hitter. He called for veteran Tony
Lazzeri, a former New York Yankee who was finishing
out his career as a Cub player-coach.

Lazzeri jumped on a curve and smashed a long
double, scoring Collins and sending Jurges to third.
Hartnett's next move was to replace the aging Lazzeri
with a pinch-runner—speedy Joe Marty. The next
man up was Chicago's best hitter, third baseman Stan
Hack, who drew a walk from the rattled Swift. With
the bases loaded and still no outs, the Pittsburgh bull
pen worked furiously in case Traynor decided to yank

Swift. But the Pirate manager hesitated, then allowed his reliever to pitch to one more man—Billy Herman.

Herman drilled a single to right, scoring Jurges. A great throw by Pirate right fielder Paul Waner cut Marty down at the plate, but the Cubs had tied the game 5–5. They still had men on first and third and only one out. That was all for Swift. Traynor waved to the bull pen for Mace Brown, his ace fireman that season. Brown immediately got Frank Demaree to hit into an inning-ending double play.

As the inning came to a close, the sky darkened and evening shadows moved across Wrigley Field. The stadium was not equipped with artificial lighting, so the umpires had to make an important decision. Should they continue the game or call it off on account of darkness? After a quick conference at home plate, the umps declared that the teams would play one more full inning—and that would be all. Play resumed.

Charlie Root, the 39-year-old senior citizen of the Chicago mound staff, pitched the ninth inning and got the side out quickly—with some assistance from the charcoal sky, which was making it difficult for the batters to see the ball.

The Cubs had just one more chance to break the tie. If they couldn't put a run together in the ninth, the game would be called. In the stands, hundreds of Cub fans nervously lit up their cigarettes, and the glowing butts twinkled like fireflies in the darkened arena. Some people actually created makeshift torches by putting matches to their scorecards. If the Cubs had to extend the inning with a time-consuming rally, a few of the fans would no doubt have been tempted to set Wrigley Field on fire to make it easier for their heroes to see the ball.

But unfortunately, it looked as if it was going to be a short inning. First Phil Cavaretta led off for the Cubs and flied out to center. Then Carl Reynolds grounded out. One more out, and the inning—and the game— would be over.

The next batter was Gabby Hartnett. It was up to him to save the day for the Cubs, and there wasn't a soul in Wrigley Field who wanted the win any more than Old Tomato Face. And yet, as Hartnett grabbed a bat and advanced to the plate, he looked like the calmest person in the park.

Pirate pitcher Mace Brown squinted into the alley leading to Al Todd's mitt, but he couldn't pick up his catcher's sign. Nevertheless, Brown's first pitch streaked right into the strike zone. Gabby swung—and missed. On Brown's second delivery, Hartnett got a piece of the ball and sent it beyond the foul line into the dark grandstand seats.

Brown served up his third pitch, a fastball with everything he had behind it. Hartnett's bat slashed through the night air, connected with the ball, and sent it zooming like a comet into the left field bleachers!

The Cub manager may have been the only one in the park who saw where the ball went. Hartnett watched it soar for two full seconds, then tossed his bat

Mobbed by admiring fans and teammates after his pennant-clinching
home run, Gabby is escorted from the field by security guards.

aside and began his trip around the bases. By the time he got to second base, the Chicago fans had poured out on the field in an explosion of enthusiasm. Gabby didn't have to walk another step after that. He was practically carried to home plate by the delirious crowd.

At the moment Gabby touched home plate, the Cubs moved into first plate, one half game ahead of the Pirates. The next afternoon Bill Lee wrapped up the series for Chicago by pitching an easy 10–1 win over the thoroughly demoralized Pirates. Then the Cubs moved on to St. Louis, where they mowed down the Cardinals on the last Saturday of the 1938 schedule. It was all over. The Chicago Cubs had won the pennant.

Few people even remember that the Cubs went on to drop four straight games to the New York Yankees in the World Series that year. But what stands out even today as one of baseball's brightest moments is the home run hit by Gabby Hartnett in the inky darkness of Wrigley Field, September 28, 1938.

NOLAN RYAN

A Season of Strikeouts

Nolan Ryan went from the Lone Star State of Texas to the National League with an innocent, country-boy look on his face and a baseball clutched in his powerful right hand. When Ryan played his first major league game in 1966, Dodger ace Sandy Koufax was finishing the twelfth and final season of his great career. Many baseball experts claimed that Koufax was the fastest pitcher of all time, and his lifetime total of 2,396 strikeouts certainly supported that claim. It was said that Sandy was faster than Walter Johnson, or Dazzy Vance, or Bob Feller . . . or anyone. But then along came Nolan Ryan.

"You can actually *hear* Ryan's fastball," said super-slugger Ron Blomberg of the New York Yankees.

"There ought to be a law against guys like him," said Blomberg's teammate, pitcher Sam McDowell.

"Ryan is a heckuva pitcher," grudgingly admitted Hall-of-Famer Bob Feller, the former Cleveland Indian strikeout ace.

Just about everyone who'd ever seen Ryan in action was awed by the big California Angel's blazing fastball. And it was that fastball that the fans in Anaheim Stadium on September 26, 1973, had come to see. As Nolan Ryan began his windup, he was only one pitch away from breaking the single-season strikeout record of 382, established by Koufax in 1965.

Nolan Ryan's right arm reared straight back and his fingers tightened against the ball. His left leg started its outward swing and his eyes locked on the gloved target just beyond the batter's knees. Whoosh! The ball streaked toward the plate in a blur, exploding into the catcher's mitt with a sharp, popping sound.

At that moment, all the years of disappointment, all the nagging shadows of doubt that had plagued Ryan's major league career were swept aside. As the ball rocketed toward the plate, his place in baseball history was finally assured.

Born in Refugio, Texas, on January 31, 1947, Nolan Ryan had been a 295th draft choice of the New York Mets in 1965. The 17-year-old rookie's first stop was Marion, Virginia, in the Appalachian League, where he struck out 115 batters in 78 innings. A year later he fanned 313 batters in 205 innings and wound up with a 17–2 record for Greenville in the Western Carolina League.

That kind of pitching earned Ryan a shot with the Mets at the tail end of the '66 season. He appeared in two games and pitched just three innings, striking out six batters and walking three. In 1967 Nolan spent a frustrating, unproductive season at Winter Haven in the Florida State League and Jacksonville in the International League.

The Mets brought him up again, in 1968—with mixed results. At first he seemed to be spending more time soaking his blistered fingers in pickle brine than pitching. When he did pitch, he experienced streaks of wildness which resulted in an abundance of walks and a 6–9 won–lost record. Still, his smoking fastball was becoming the talk of the league. Striking out 133 batters in a total of 134 innings, he often seemed to be on the verge of greatness. Met fans began to rate him with the ace of the staff, Tom Seaver. Some even predicted that he would eventually surpass Walter Johnson's lifetime record of 3,506 strikeouts.

But three years later Ryan's career with the Mets was rudely halted. In his four full seasons with the New Yorkers, he had shown unlimited potential and definite flashes of brilliance. Nevertheless, his disappointing 29–37 total won–lost record made manager Gil Hodges doubt that Ryan would ever really live up to his potential. So on December 10, 1971, the Mets traded Nolan to the California Angels for third baseman Jim Fregosi.

"I'll never forget how I felt when the trading deadline neared," Ryan recalled. "I wanted to be traded, but I was hesitant. You never know what's going to be best for your future."

It didn't take Ryan long to find out. He got off to a fine start with the Angels and finished the 1972 campaign with a league-leading 329 strikeouts, a fantastic 2.28 earned run average and a 19–16 won–lost record, his best effort yet. There was no question about it: While Fregosi was fighting off nagging injuries and contributing a mediocre .232 batting average to the Mets, the Nolan Ryan Express was roaring toward greatness.

Nolan really put it all together the next year. On May 15, 1973, against the Royals in Kansas City, he pitched his first no-hitter, giving up only three walks while collecting twelve strikeouts.

Angel catcher Jeff Torborg, who caught for Ryan that night, had a ringside seat for the dramatic event. "Nolan had great stuff, right up there with Koufax," he raved. A hard man to impress, Torborg was an old hand at no-hitters. As a Dodger, he had handled Sandy's perfect game against the Cubs in 1965.

Two months later, on July 15, Ryan notched his second no-hitter of the year, striking out 17 Detroit Tigers in the process. By then he was moving down the strikeout trail with breathtaking speed. By mid-August he had 288 strikeouts, and by September 19, he had passed the 350 mark.

As the '73 campaign wound down, Ryan began making a serious bid for the major league strikeout record of 382, set by Koufax in the 1965 season. And

Pitching for the New York Mets in 1971, Nolan Ryan showed moments of greatness—and streaks of wildness.

on September 23, Ryan fanned twelve Minnesota Twins, bringing his season's total to 367—just 15 short of the magic number.

But time was running out for Nolan. The season was drawing to a close, and he had just one more chance to make his mark. His final pitching effort of the year would take place on September 26, against Minnesota once again. He needed 15 strikeouts in that game to tie the record—one more to go out in front. It was a real long-shot, even for a strikeout artist like Ryan, but the Angel ace was determined to give it a try.

Only 9,000 fans showed up at Anaheim Stadium on September 26, as Ryan made his last-ditch attempt for the record. Ryan got off to a fast start. Throughout the early innings, one Minnesota batter after another went down before his overpowering serves. Then, in the eighth inning, Steve Brye went down on a 2–2 pitch and the fans scattered around the vast arena rose to their feet and began to cheer. For with that strikeout— his 382nd of the season—Nolan Ryan had finally caught up with Sandy Koufax. And at the rate he was going, Ryan seemed sure to pull ahead before the game ended.

But trouble was just around the corner. In the ninth inning, Nolan developed a cramp in his right hamstring muscle. Suddenly, he lost some of his concentration and most of the steam off his fastball and curve. He didn't get a single strikeout in the ninth. Luckily the game was tied and went into extra innings. But Ryan failed to get a strikeout in the tenth, and he seemed to be tiring rapidly.

In the top of the eleventh inning, Angel manager Bobby Winkles strode to the mound to talk to Ryan. The fans stirred uneasily in their seats. If Winkles yanked his star right-hander now, it would be the end of Ryan's quest for the all-time record.

But when Winkles asked him how he felt, the big Texan confidently replied, "I've got enough left to strike out one more guy." Winkles just grinned and headed back to the dugout. With a quick look at the scoreboard, then a check of his defenses, Ryan coolly turned to face the next batter.

At the plate was Rich Reese, who had entered the game as a pinch-runner for Harmon Killebrew in the ninth. Nolan's first pitch whipped in as if jet-propelled.

After being traded to the Los Angeles Angels, Ryan really came into his own in 1973. Here he rejoices after his first no-hitter.

Ryan delivers the fastball that gave him his 383rd strikeout for the 1973 season—and the all-time major league record.

When the umpire signaled a strike, the Angel fans jumped up and down and shot their fists in the air. They seemed to sense the energy that had suddenly flowed back into Ryan's arm, and now they wanted to let him know they were with him.

Ryan's next pitch was a carbon copy of his first— right over the plate, with speed to spare.

Ryan flicked a bead of sweat from his brow, studied Reese momentarily, and then went into his windup.

The ball made a loud thud as it landed in the catcher's glove, the umpire bellowed, "Strike three!" and Rich Reese dazedly left the batter's box. He was the 16th strikeout victim of the game and the 383rd batter to go down on strikes that season against Nolan Ryan, the new strikeout king!

It almost seemed anticlimactic when the Angels won the game 5–4 in the bottom of the eleventh. The real story that night was not about a team effort but about an incredible one-man show. Ryan's final performance had capped off a super-season, and in addition to his new strikeout record he now had several other lines to add to the record book. The statisticians worked overtime to compile them all:

Major league record for total strikeouts in two consecutive seasons—712 (old modern mark 699, Koufax).

Major league record for ten or more strikeouts in a game—23 times (old mark, 21, Koufax).

Major league record for strikeouts in three consecutive games—41 in 27 innings (shared by Koufax and Luis Tiant, both in 28 innings).

American League record for strikeouts in two consecutive games—30 in 18 innings (shared by Sam McDowell).

To top it all off, Ryan also became the fourth man ever to pitch two no-hit victories in one season and the third to strike out 300 batters two years in a row. Equally important to Ryan was the fact that he'd finally made it into the 20-game winners' circle, finishing the season with a 21–16 won–lost record.

"I remember once talking with Tom Seaver about the strikeout record held by Koufax," Ryan later explained. "We both thought nobody would ever break it. Well, now that I have, I'm very pleased. But I'm also glad to have 21 wins, too. It wouldn't mean as much if I'd only won 19 games."

FRED MERKLE

The Bonehead Play

Fred Tenney felt the pain as soon as he woke up. The dull, throbbing pain caused the New York Giant first baseman to grunt and fall back wearily on his bed. Tenney had been suffering from lumbago for years, but this was the most severe attack he'd ever had. And it couldn't have happened on a worse day. Tenney cursed his aching back as he realized that it would be impossible to play in the big game that afternoon.

It was Wednesday, September 23, 1908. A hard-fought National League pennant race was grinding to a finish, and the Giants were barely in first place—just six percentage points ahead of the Chicago Cubs. New York and Chicago were in the midst of a critical four-game series. The Giants had lost the first two games, 4–3 and 3–1, and now they needed a victory in

57

the third game to keep them on top in their sputtering drive to a World Series berth.

Tenney knew his teammates were counting on his help in this all-important contest, but there was nothing he could do about it. So he rose unsteadily from his bed, got dressed, and headed for the Polo Grounds to give his manager, John McGraw, the bad news.

John McGraw was one of baseball's greatest managers. He had begun his own baseball career in 1891 as a shortstop with the Baltimore club of the American Association. In 1902 he had taken over as player-manager of the Giants and had led them to the top of the league.

When Tenney reached the ballpark he went straight to the manager's office. "I'm sorry, Mister McGraw," he said sadly. "The lumbago is acting up something fierce. I just can't make it today."

The peppery little manager clamped his jaws shut for an instant. Tenney was a veteran of 15 major league campaigns, a brilliant fielder, and a steady hitter. In fact, the first baseman was leading the league in runs scored that season. He would not be an easy man to replace.

McGraw considered several possible substitutes and finally said, "Well, I guess I'll go with young Merkle."

Fred Merkle was 19 years old, practically a raw rookie. Since joining the Giants in 1907, he had appeared in only 15 games. Born in Watertown, Wisconsin, Merkle was still awed by the big city and

Young Fred Merkle was called on to substitute for Giant veteran Fred Tenney during the hot National League pennant race in 1908.

his big league teammates. But McGraw liked the
youngster's attitude—his hustle—and expected Merkle
to go far some day. In fact, he had originally signed
Merkle as a possible successor to the aging Tenney.

Nevertheless, when the starting line-ups for the
crucial game against the Cubs were announced, Fred
Merkle's name set off a disheartened murmur in the
Polo Grounds stands. The Giant faithful knew what
Tenney could do, but they still weren't sure about
Merkle.

The fans settled down when the Giant nine took up
their positions on the field. Above the roar of 25,000
rooters, plate umpire Hank O'Day bellowed out the
familiar cry of "Play Ball!" O'Day adjusted his mask,
dug his spikes into the ground behind the catcher, and
made a mental note to keep everything before him in
sharp focus.

The first Cub batter stepped to the plate. On the
mound for New York was Christy Mathewson, the
Giant ace. For years a consistent 20- and 30-game
winner, Mathewson was having his best season ever.
But today he would be facing Cub Jack Pfeister, a
southpaw with a growing reputation as a Giant killer.
Mathewson touched the rubber and peered in for a
sign. And Fred Merkle, stationed at first base, took a
deep breath, then gave his mitt a couple of taps for
good luck.

Inning after inning, both Pfeister and Mathewson
set down the opposition with relative ease. Tension in
the Giant ballpark began to build in rising waves as

the fans waited to see which pitcher would crack first.

Finally, in the top of the fifth, Cub shortstop Joe Tinker got the fat part of his bat on a Mathewson pitch and drove the ball past outfielder Mike Donlin, who made a desperate lunge for it. Tinker sped around the bases for an inside-the-park home run, giving Chicago a 1–0 lead. But Donlin redeemed himself in the bottom of the sixth by driving home Giant infielder Buck Herzog to tie up the score.

The game was still deadlocked when the Giants came to bat in the last of the ninth. Cy Seymour hit a ground ball to second baseman Johnny Evers for the first out, but Artie Devlin brought the crowd to its feet with a single. Moose McCormick then smashed a hard grounder at Evers, who handled the ball with ease, forcing Devlin at second with a quick toss to shortstop Joe Tinker. Then with two men down and McCormick on first base, young Fred Merkle advanced to the plate.

High up in the stands sat Fred Tenney. Unnoticed in his street clothes, the pain-wracked Giant first baseman had been nervously watching the big game. Now he stood up and implored his substitute, Fred Merkle, to get a piece of the ball—to get on base and keep the Giant hopes alive.

Merkle couldn't have heard the veteran's pleas, but he came through anyway. The young Giant lashed a clothesline single just fair down the right-field foul line, sending McCormick to third base and everyone else at the Polo Grounds into a state of euphoria.

Now it was up to shortstop Al Bridwell to get McCormick home with the winning run. Bridwell had come to New York that year after three seasons with Cincinnati and Boston. Standing only 5-foot-9 and weighing 170 pounds, the little Giant took a big swing and rifled a Pfeister pitch over second, sending McCormick in with the tie-breaking run that evidently put the Giants a full game ahead of the second-place Cubs.

As McCormick dashed across home plate, the Polo Grounds exploded with cheers and the fans spilled out of the stands to engulf their heroes. Fred Merkle, thrilled to have played an important part in the great Giant rally, disappeared into a sea of well-wishers.

In the midst of all the confusion, no one noticed that Chicago's Johnny Evers was frantically waving to outfielder Solly Hofman, who was still in possession of the ball hit by Bridwell. "Throw the ball, Solly . . ." shouted Evers.

The Chicago infielder had good reason to call for the ball. For Merkle, in his excitement and eagerness to get off the playing field ahead of the crowd, had pulled up short of second base and dashed for the dugout as soon as McCormick had touched home. Evers was shrewd enough to know that if he could get the ball and touch second, Merkle could still be forced out and the winning run would not count.

Strangely enough, only three weeks earlier, Evers had been involved in a similar incident in a game against Pittsburgh. After everyone assumed the Pirates had scored the winning run, Evers had gotten the ball

and touched second to force out the base runner from
first. That time, however, umpire Hank O'Day had
ruled that the run counted anyway. But in the heated
dispute that followed, Evers had proved that according
to the rule book, if a runner is on first when a hit is
made, he *must* touch second no matter what. If he
doesn't, he can be forced out. Furthermore, if that out
is the third of the inning, any runs scored on the play
do not count.

Now, since the same Hank O'Day was the chief
umpire in this game against the Giants, Evers knew
that if he could get the ball and touch second base, the
ump would have to rule Merkle out on the play and
send the game into extra innings.

Solly Hofman heard Evers shout for the ball, but he
couldn't see his second baseman too well. Evers was all
but hidden by the jubilant crowd. Confused, Hofman
fired an erratic heave toward first base. The ball
bounced past Evers and into the hands of Giant
player-coach Joe McGinnity. McGinnity clung to the
ball as if his life depended on it, refusing to give it up
even when Chicago shortstop Joe Tinker climbed on
his back in a desperate attempt to wrestle the ball
away.

Cub manager Frank Chance also got into the fray.
Spotting Hank O'Day in the crowd, he spun his arms
around like a windmill. "Didn't you see that?" he
shrieked at the umpire. "Merkle never touched second!"

Meanwhile, McGinnity had managed to shake

Tinker off his back. Once free, the Giant player-coach cranked up his right arm and propelled the ball in the general direction of third base, where it was picked up by a spectator. Second string Cub pitcher Rube Kroh, following the action, hustled over to the fan and demanded the ball.

"Not on your life," shot back the fan, whereupon Kroh allegedly leveled him with a well-placed blow to the jaw and retrieved the ball. Kroh then threw the most important toss of his pitching career. The ball went straight into the glove of Evers, who stepped on second base!

Once again, exactly as had happened three weeks earlier, Evers raised his voice above the din. "That's the third out!" he cried. "The run doesn't count!"

After hurriedly consulting with fellow umpire Robert Emslie, O'Day decided that indeed the run *did not* count. But it was too late to do anything more about the situation. The Giant fans were still milling all over the field, and those who heard the ruling grew ugly in mood. A full-scale riot seemed more than possible as the crowd turned toward O'Day.

The park police rescued the rattled umpire in the nick of time, hustling him away from danger and into the safety of the dressing room. But before he departed, O'Day had one last word for all. "I declare this game a tie!" he said.

Questioned by reporters minutes later, O'Day admitted that he hadn't been able to *see* the action but had ruled a force because he *presumed* Merkle hadn't touched second base. He went on to say that since the spectators had completely overrun the field of play, it would have been impossible to let the game continue into the tenth inning.

Another version of the controversial play was given by another on-the-scene witness. According to Giant manager John McGraw, Evers had successfully gotten away with a brilliant trick.

"Evers never even got the ball," the Giant skipper insisted. "It rolled through the crowd and passed third base. Kroh grabbed the ball, but McGinnity snatched it from Kroh and threw it into the left-field bleachers. Evers never *had* the ball! He just grabbed one of the spare balls from O'Day's pocket, ran to second, stepped on it, and demanded that Merkle be called out."

National League president Harry Pulliam had been in the stands during the remarkable contest, and that evening he backed up O'Day's ruling: Merkle was out, McCormick's run didn't count, and the game would be considered a tie.

The Giants took one last step to salvage a victory. They appealed Pulliam's ruling to the National League board of directors—but to no avail. The board upheld Pulliam's decision. The Giants and Cubs would replay the game at the end of the season, they added, *if* it had a bearing on the final outcome of the pennant race.

In the closing days of the schedule, both teams struggled for sole possession of first place, but on the

Chicago's Johnny Evers (above) started the Merkle controversy—and umpire Hank O'Day (opposite) had the last word.

final day of the regular season they finished with
identical 98–55 records. The tie game of September 23
would have to be replayed!

On October 8, some 35,000 people jammed the Polo
Grounds to watch the showdown between the two
clubs. In another thriller, Mordecai "Three-Finger"
Brown came in as a relief pitcher for the Cubs and
outdueled Christy Mathewson. The Cubs won 4–2 to
squeak past the Giants for the 1908 National League
pennant. The Cubs went on to win the World Series
crown, easily beating the Detroit Tigers four games to
one. The Giants finally captured the pennant in 1911,
but then they were defeated in the Series by the
Philadelphia A's.

As for Fred Merkle, the fans never forgot his blunder
on that fateful September afternoon in 1908. For the
rest of his playing days, he was tagged with the
inglorious name of "Bonehead."

Through it all, Merkle gave a good account of
himself, going on to play 18 more seasons in the
majors. In a total of 1,638 games, he maintained a
lifetime batting average of .273, racking up 1,580 hits,
290 doubles, 81 triples, 60 home runs, and 733 RBI's.
But no matter how well he did, he was always plagued
by that one "Bonehead" play.

In 1926 Merkle retired and headed south for some
well-earned peace and solitude. But even then, he was
never allowed to forget his big blunder. Although he
spent many happy hours gazing out at the blue waters

that sparkled in the Florida sun, his rest would invariably be interrupted by some passing stranger.

"Say, aren't you *the* Fred Merkle?" the stranger would ask. "You know . . . the one who committed the bonehead play?"

And smiling wistfully, Merkle would nod.

Whereupon the stranger would likely ask, "How did it feel, Mr. Merkle, when you realized you forgot to touch second base?"

Merkle could remember the play as clearly as if it had happened the day before . . . when he was only 19 years old . . . when it was great to be young and a Giant . . . .

"When the meaning of it suddenly dawned upon me," Fred Merkle told all the passing strangers who ever asked him the question, "I wished that a large, roomy, and comfortable hole would open up and swallow me."

TED WILLIAMS

Breaking the .400 Barrier

From the time he was a boy, Ted Williams wanted to be the greatest hitter who ever lived. "When I was a kid," he said years later, "I wished it on every star . . . that I could be the hitter I wanted to be."

But Ted did more than wish—much more. Throughout his childhood and during his 19 years with the Boston Red Sox, he devoted almost all his time and energy to making that dream come true.

Born in San Diego, California, on August 30, 1918, Theodore Samuel Williams grew up in a climate where the sun was always warm and a boy could play baseball nearly every day of the year.

"When I was growing up, between the ages of nine and seventeen, all I did was learn hitting," Williams recalled. "From morning to night."

Ted's dedication paid off, and in 1936, at the age 17,

he signed a contract with the San Diego Padres of the Pacific Coast League. At first, manager Frank Shellenback used Ted as a pitcher. But when the 145-pound, 6-foot-3 youngster delivered a pinch-hit double off the fence in an early league contest, Shellenback wisely moved Ted to the outfield and told him to concentrate on hitting.

Two years later Williams moved to the Minneapolis club of the American Association, where he led the Triple A league with a .366 batting average that included 43 home runs and 142 runs batted in.

Ted became a major leaguer the following year, 1939, when the Boston Red Sox bought his contract from Minneapolis. Bosox player-manager Joe Cronin felt the 20-year-old rookie might add some punch to an already intimidating line-up. Among the Boston regulars were such super-sluggers as Jimmy Foxx, Bobby Doerr, Doc Cramer, Joe Vosmik, and Cronin himself.

Most young rookies would have been awed to find themselves in such impressive company. But Williams was a pretty good hitter himself. One morning during spring training, Ted was taking his turn at the batting cage, when second baseman Bobby Doerr decided to needle the rookie slugger.

"Hey, kid," Doerr said, "wait'll you see Foxx hit."

Ted knew that Jimmy Foxx was one of the game's best hitters. But without taking his eye off the next pitch, he snapped back, "Wait'll Foxx sees *me* hit!" and proceeded to knock the ball over the right-field fence.

Boston rookie Ted Williams belts one out at the Red Sox spring training camp in 1939.

Williams' confidence in his ability to hit the ball was well founded, as he proved during his fabulous rookie season. Working day and night to perfect his swing, studying the opposing pitchers, and building his skinny frame up to maximum strength, Williams soon became the talk of the entire Red Sox camp. And it wasn't long before every baseball buff in America knew his name. Williams finished the '39 season—his first in the majors—with a sensational .326 batting average, 31 home runs, and a league-leading 145 RBI's.

In 1940 Ted's statistics were even more impressive. His average climbed to .344, and he scored more runs than any hitter in the league. In just two years Ted Williams had established himself as an outstanding major leaguer. And no one doubted that this was just the beginning for "The Splendid Splinter," as the tall, thin slugger was nicknamed.

Ted and his fans were expecting even bigger and better things in 1941. But during spring training Williams chipped a bone in his ankle. The injury forced him out of the regular line-up, and it seemed possible that he might well be hobbled for the whole season. But Ted fought off the pain and managed to get out to the park every morning for batting practice. Day after day he sharpened his batting eye against Red Sox pitcher Joe Dobson. Dobson threw his best curves and fastballs at Ted, and The Splinter responded by belting them all over the park.

Slowly, Ted worked his way back into the batting order as a pinch-hitter. Then, as the days got warmer, his ankle mended and he was able to take on full-time duties at the plate and on the field. Fully recovered in May, Ted began racking up hits at a record rate. By June his batting average had hit a high-water mark of .436. But could he possibly keep it up?

In 1930, New York Giant Bill Terry had averaged .401 for a full season, but no one had reached the .400 mark since. The last American League player to accomplish the feat was Detroit's Harry Heilmann, who hit .403 for the Tigers in 1923.

It seemed unlikely that anyone would ever bat .400 again. Baseball techniques had improved dramatically since Terry's triumph. And the pitching had been refined to the point of near perfection. In 1941 there were a lot of brilliant hurlers in the American League like Lefty Gomez, Red Ruffing, Tommy Bridges, Bob Feller, Ted Lyons, Dutch Leonard, Bobo Newsom, and Johnny Allen. But Williams wasn't worried about them.

Ted maintained his .400 pace all through June and into July. Then came the All-Star game, which he won for the American League with a ninth-inning homer. After the All-Star break, Williams pressed forward, determined to become the first .400 hitter since Bill Terry. By August he was still going strong, but the pressure was beginning to build.

Ted asked a few old-time batting champs for advice. One of them was Hugh Duffy, a Red Sox coach who had hit .438 in 1894. Duffy liked Ted's natural stance at the plate and urged him not to change a thing.

"Son, you've got form and power," said Duffy. "But form is most important. With it you get the power. Don't monkey with your form."

When the Red Sox traveled to Detroit, Ted also talked to Harry Heilmann. The man who had once hit .403 was now happy to go over batting theories with the young Red Sox star. "Just hit the ball where you want it," Heilmann suggested. "Hit your pitch; get your base hits. You can hit .400. You can do it."

Williams did concentrate on getting base hits, but along with the stream of singles and doubles, he also led the Red Sox in home runs and RBI's. Ted hit his

Teammates during the 1941 All-Star game, Williams and Joe DiMaggio were rivals the rest of the season.

way through August at a steady clip, and by mid-September his .400 season seemed almost assured. But suddenly, as the season fell away to the last few games in September, Williams went into a slump. Points melted off his average at an alarming rate, and by September 28 (the last day of the '41 season) it had shrunk to .39955.

Officially, his average would be rounded off to an even .400, so manager Joe Cronin gave Ted the option of sitting out the season-ending doubleheader against the Philadelphia Athletics. "It's up to you," Cronin told Williams that morning. "Do you want to play or sit it out?"

"I don't want anybody to say I got in through the back door," Williams replied. "I'll play."

September 28 was a cold, damp afternoon in Philadelphia, but 10,000 fans turned out to watch Ted Williams take his final cuts of the year. Everyone realized that each swing could make—or break—his .400 season.

Philadelphia manager Connie Mack had selected right-hander Dick Fowler to pitch the opener, and as Williams came up to bat in the first inning, catcher Frankie Hayes was squatting behind the plate.

"Listen, Ted," Hayes whispered from behind his mask, "Mister Mack told us if we let up on you, he'll run us out of baseball. I wish you all the luck in the world, but we're not giving you a darn thing."

Home plate umpire Bill McGowen then stepped over the plate to dust it off. "To hit .400 a batter has got to be loose," mumbled McGowen, brushing some dirt away with his whisk broom.

Williams couldn't have been looser as he measured a Fowler curve and drove it into right field for a single. His second time up and still against Fowler, The Splinter exploded one of the longest drives he had ever hit for his 37th home run of the season. When he came to the plate for his third appearance, reliever Porter Vaughan was on the mound. Williams promptly made Vaughan skip rope with a liner through the box for his third hit. And later, with Vaughan still pitching, Ted got his fourth straight hit of the day—a clothesline single over first baseman Bob Johnson's head.

With four hits in the first game, Williams had it made. All he had to do was sit out the second game and the rest would be history. But that wasn't Ted's style. He told Cronin that he had to play in the second half of the doubleheader. Only then would he be satisfied that the .400 average was really his.

Fred Caligiuri started the second contest for Philadelphia and went all the way to a 7–1 win over the Sox. But the score seemed almost insignificant. What really counted was Ted Williams. From the start of game two, even the Philadelphia fans began cheering wildly each time he marched to the plate. Three times Ted came up, and twice he connected—first for a single and then for a double.

Altogether, Williams batted eight times and collected six hits in the doubleheader. That made his official batting average for the season a sensational .406! Few could doubt that Ted's dream of becoming baseball's greatest hitter was finally coming true.

Many baseball fans considered Williams a shoo-in for the American League's Most Valuable Player award, but he wasn't the only player to have a great season. That same year, Joe DiMaggio had hit safely in 56 consecutive games. Joltin' Joe's accomplishment was recognized as one of the most remarkable achievements in the history of the game, and DiMaggio walked off with the MVP award.

As for Williams, he went on to win five more batting

Still going strong in 1955, 37-year-old Ted Williams shows the form that made him baseball's greatest hitter.

titles and two MVP awards before hanging up his spikes in 1960. Ted, then 42 years old, finished his last major league season with a .316 average.

Six years after his retirement, baseball paid a lasting tribute to Williams. By virtue of his .406 average in 1941, his lifetime average of .344, and countless other batting feats during his magnificent career with the Boston Red Sox, Ted Williams was elected to the Hall of Fame. There would be many great hitters in the years to come, but few—if any—would rival The Splendid Splinter.

LOU GEHRIG

A Sad Farewell

In an early spring game at Yankee Stadium—April 30, 1939—Washington Senator pitcher Joe Krakauskas threw a fastball that should have chased New York Yankee batter Lou Gehrig away from the plate. Instead, Gehrig leaned into the inside pitch. If the fabled Yankee hero had leaned in another inch, the ball would have knocked him down.

"You know," Krakauskas confided to a teammate between innings, "I could swear Gehrig took one of my pitches inside his wrists . . . in the loop formed by his arms. Weirdest thing I ever saw."

Krakauskas wasn't the only one to notice something unusual about the great Yankee slugger that day. Gehrig had come up to bat four times, and four times he had left men on base. Not once had he managed to get the ball out of the infield.

As the 23,712 fans filed out of the stadium after the Yankees' 3–2 loss, many of them shook their heads in disbelief. They had never seen the Yankee batting king look so bad at the plate—or in the field, for that matter.

"Did you see how he moved on that dribbler down the first-base line?" asked one strap-hanger of another on the subway ride back home after the game.

"Sure," said his fellow fan. "It was the kind of ground ball that Lou would've put in his hip pocket a year or two ago. I guess he's just getting old."

Gehrig would soon be 36 years old, which could have explained the gradual slowing down of his reflexes. But there were other disturbing signs that *couldn't* be explained simply by age. For years Gehrig had been an outstanding first baseman, a sure-handed fielder who worked very hard to master his position. On the rare occasions that he did make an error, the official scorer usually had to think twice before signaling the scoreboard people to flash an "E" sign. Therefore, one particular incident during that Yankee–Senator game of April 30 stood out as a sad example of Gehrig's almost total collapse as a ball player.

A Washington batter had slapped a one-hop grounder between the pitcher's mound and first base. Yankee hurler Oral Hildenbrand had fielded the ball, dashed toward first, and flipped an underhand throw to Gehrig—who had dropped the easy toss. The official scorer had hesitated, then ruled the play a hit, obviously trying to save Gehrig from further embarrassment. But the miscue was so glaring that even a few of the most ardent Gehrig supporters had booed the decision.

Gehrig knew as well as anyone that something was wrong. That just wasn't the kind of ball the Yankee veteran was used to playing. In his 16 years in the majors, Gehrig had emerged as one of baseball's brightest stars. His glorious career had started in 1923, when the scared, painfully self-conscious rookie had first joined the Yankees. In those days, Babe Ruth had ruled supreme in the major leagues. Surrounded by other great Yankee batters, Ruth had made the New Yorkers the dominant team in the American League. Among the Yankee stars, Wally Pipp was hailed as the greatest Yankee first baseman of all time. The young Gehrig had naturally been in awe of his famous teammates.

On June 1, 1925, Lou Gehrig made what appeared to be an insignificant appearance as a pinch-hitter for shortstop Pee Wee Wanninger. Yet, it turned out to be a notable moment in baseball history because it marked the beginning of an incredible consecutive game streak that Lou Gehrig would compile over the next 14 years.

The following day, Wally Pipp reported to Yankee Stadium complaining of a splitting headache. He had been getting them with increasing frequency—ever since he'd been hit on the head with a pitched ball during spring training. Pipp sought out trainer Doc

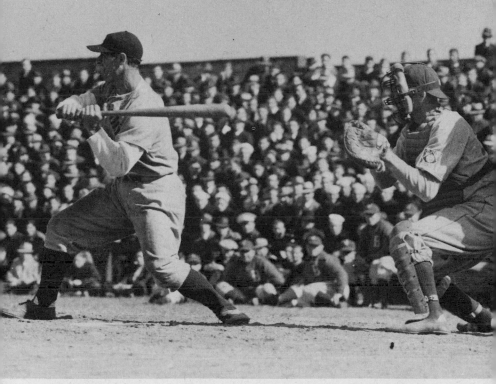

On April 14, 1939, Lou Gehrig makes one of his last appearances as a major leaguer.

Woods and asked him for a couple of aspirins. As Doc handed the pain-killer to the first baseman, Yankee manager Miller Huggins passed by.

"What's wrong, Wally?" asked Huggins.

"It's another one of those headaches," answered Pipp. "A real bad one, I'm afraid."

"Why don't you take the day off?" Huggins asked sympathetically. "Let's see what young Gehrig can do."

When the starting Yankee line-up was announced that day, Lou Gehrig was at first base. His big chance had come, and he wanted to make the most of it. Nervously, he faced George Mogridge of the Senators. Lou overcame his nervousness well enough to reach the tall southpaw for a double and two singles. Huggins was so impressed with Gehrig that he put the big, awkward rookie back on first base the following day. In fact, Wally Pipp never again played first base for the Yankees.

As the years rolled by, Gehrig became a highly skilled, graceful guardian of his position. And he was even more impressive at the plate. In his first full season, Gehrig hit .295, and his batting average soared to the high .300s in the years that followed. And when it came to home runs, the powerful Yank was soon belting out 30 and 40 a year. By 1935, when the Sultan of Swat, Babe Ruth, left the team to play with the Boston Braves, Gehrig had become the dominant figure in the major leagues. And in all those years, never once did he miss a Yankee ball game.

Game after game, he improved his skills in the field and in the batter's box. In the winter months, when most players relaxed after the exhausting 154-game schedule, Lou spent hours each day, hiking and ice skating to keep fit. And once the season started again, he played ball day in and day out. Neither colds nor charley horses, bruised muscles nor strained ligaments could keep him out of the line-up. At the peak of his career in 1936, Lou Gehrig was known as the Iron

At the peak of his career in the early 1930s, Lou clowns for the camera during spring training.

Horse because of his incredible strength and endurance.

Going into the '39 season, Gehrig's batting records and outstanding fielding made him a sure-fire candidate for the Hall of Fame. He had led his league twice in home runs and was the RBI champion five times. Altogether, Lou had collected 493 home runs, 2,717 hits, and 1,989 RBI's. His lifetime batting average was .340.

But as the 1939 season got underway, Gehrig hardly seemed like himself. He had suffered a few bouts of illness during the previous season, and his coordination had sometimes seemed a little bit off. But things had gotten even worse since then. In the first eight games of '39, Gehrig had only four singles to show for 28 times at bat, and his average had plummeted to an embarrassing .143. Now, after his disastrous showing at the April 30 game, Gehrig knew he had some serious thinking to do.

Lou and his wife Eleanor spent the following day in seclusion. There were things to discuss, decisions to be made. It was Monday, a day off for the Yankees, and the Gehrigs spent it talking about the past—and the future. They talked about the many pleasures they had shared in past seasons and the hard reality of Lou's present condition. And by the time the sun went down beyond the trees outside their home, Lou Gehrig knew what he had to do.

The Yankees were scheduled to open a series against the Tigers the following day, May 2. As he entered the lobby of his hotel in Detroit that morning, the Iron Horse was satisfied that the decision he had made the day before was the right one. He had achieved almost everything he had wished for when he first put on his Yankee uniform in 1923. And now, after 2,130 straight games, it was time for him to quit.

Gehrig had been in touch with his manager, Joe McCarthy, and the Yankee skipper had flown to Detroit to meet with his aging star. As the two men greeted each other in the lobby, they exchanged strained pleasantries, then went up to Gehrig's room.

As soon as McCarthy settled into a chair, Gehrig cleared his throat and spoke the fateful words. "Joe, I always said that when I felt I couldn't help the team any more, I would take myself out of the line-up," he said. "I guess the time has come."

"Are you sure this is what you want?" McCarthy asked sadly.

"I've thought it all out," replied Gehrig. "I've been wrestling with this ever since Sunday. I'm no good to the club, to myself, to the fans, to the game, or to you."

"When do you want to quit?" McCarthy asked.

Gehrig never wavered. "Now. Put Babe Dahlgren in."

McCarthy lowered his head, gulped, mumbled a few words of affection, then got up and closed the door softly behind him. Alone in the room, Gehrig broke down and wept.

As team captain, Gehrig walked out to home plate at Briggs Stadium in Detroit that afternoon, handed the batting order slip to umpire Basil, then sat down in the corner of the Yankee dugout to watch Babe Dahlgren take his place in the batter's box and at first base. It was the first time in 2,130 games that Lou would watch a Yankee game from the sidelines. Aware of the significance of Gehrig's absence, his teammates saluted the Iron Horse by blitzing the Tigers 22–2.

On July 4, 1939, a Lou Gehrig Appreciation Day was held at Yankee Stadium to honor the man who had done so much for his team—and for baseball. By then, every one of the 60,000 fans jammed into Yankee Stadium knew that Gehrig had contracted a rare and incurable disease called amytrophic lateral sclerosis.

The old Yankees—the famous Murderers' Row— had come back to say farewell to Lou, and they lined up on one side of the plate. Although Babe Ruth and Lou had never been close during their many years as teammates, the immortal Babe now stood uneasily before the vast audience with the rest of the group, his eyes filled with tears. On the other side of the plate stood the new Yankees, men like Joe DiMaggio, Bill Dickey, Charlie Keller, Joe Gordon, and Red Ruffing.

There were farewell speeches by New York's Mayor LaGuardia and other dignitaries. Then Lou Gehrig approached the microphone. In the few weeks since he'd stopped playing, Gehrig's condition had deteriorated noticeably. Now as he stood before his fans and friends, the Iron Horse looked terribly weak and frail. In a soft, shaky voice, the former Yankee paid tribute to his family and all the players who had meant so

After appearing in 2,130 consecutive games, the Yankees' Iron Horse watches his teammates from the bench on May 2, 1939.

much to him. And then he looked about the Stadium and said his final words.

"You've been reading about my bad breaks for weeks now," he said. "But today I consider myself the luckiest man on the face of the earth."

Two years later, on June 2, 1941, exactly 16 years after he began his amazing 2,130 consecutive game streak, Henry Louis Gehrig died in his sleep. But memories of the Yankees' Iron Horse would live forever in the hearts of baseball fans all over the nation.

SANDY **K**OUFAX

A Perfect Game

His fastball was a white blur between the mound and the catcher's glove; his curve ball crackled at almost a right angle into the strike zone; and on each pitch, his pinpoint control seemed radar-directed. All in all, Sandy Koufax was the most dominating pitcher in the major leagues during the mid-1960s. In that short period of baseball history, he mastered the science of pitching, smashing one record after another and establishing new standards for big league hurlers.

And yet, Sandy's career began with something less than the promise of greatness. The tall, gawky left-hander was only 19 years old when he decided to try out for his hometown Dodgers. The year was 1955, and the Dodgers' ballpark was Ebbets Field in Brooklyn, New York. The team boasted a powerful array of

batters—Pee Wee Reese, Jackie Robinson, Carl Fur-
illo, Duke Snider, Gil Hodges, and Roy Campanella.
The pitching talent consisted of Don Newcombe,
Johnny Podres, Joe Black, Clem Labine, and Carl
Erskine.

Koufax had played some sandlot ball and performed
briefly as a first baseman for Lafayette High School in
Brooklyn before accepting a basketball scholarship at
the University of Cincinnati. Earlier in '55 the New
York Giants had invited him to a tryout. But Sandy's
warm-up pitches were so wild that the Giant coach
suggested he stick to basketball. And now he was about
to throw his first tryout serves to Dodger reserve
catcher Rube Walker in the familiar confines of Ebbets
Field.

Some pitches exploded into Walker's mitt as if shot
from a cannon. Others, equally fast, smashed uncon-
trollably against the batting cage. The young Koufax
knew only one pitch—his super-fastball. But, unfortunately, he never knew in what direction it would go.

Dodger manager Walter Alston looked on as Sandy
unloaded his pitches in the general direction of the
catcher. After a few minutes, he signaled Koufax to
stop. Alston had seen enough. On a hunch, he
recommended that the club sign the wild teenaged
fireballer to a $20,000 bonus, no-cut contract.

Koufax happily signed the contract and reported for
spring training. He soon learned that a pitcher needed
more than a fastball to make it in the majors. Control
was the key word there.

Sandy Koufax, the great Dodger southpaw, fires a blazing fastball.

Sandy spent most of his rookie year pitching to his teammates during batting practice, slowly learning the mechanics of his trade. The few times he did get into a game, he went to extremes. He pitched two complete game shutouts, fanning 14 batters in one contest. But in his other three starts, he had to be relieved because of his wildness. Appearing in twelve games that year, Koufax pitched a total of $41\frac{2}{3}$ innings and struck out 30 batters while giving up 28 walks.

Alston refused to give up on his wild, unpolished discovery, even though Koufax showed little progress during the next two seasons. Used as a spot pitcher during his first three seasons, Sandy won a total of nine games while losing ten.

In 1958 the Dodgers headed west to Los Angeles, and Koufax became a regular starter. The story was the same. He struck out a lot of batters, walked a lot of batters, and unknowingly intimidated many more with his glaring lack of control. In his first three years in Los Angeles, he produced mediocre 11–11, 8–6, and 8–13 records. Despite his obvious potential, it was beginning to look as if Sandy Koufax was just another promising kid who would never learn to harness his talent.

Fortunately, the turning point for Sandy was just ahead. One day in the spring of 1961, the young southpaw was having an especially hard time controlling his fastball. After watching Koufax struggle for a while, his teammate Norm Sherry finally offered some advice.

"Listen, Sandy," the second-string Dodger catcher said, "why don't you try slowing down your fastball just a bit? It would be easier to control and would still be faster than anyone else's. And why don't you go to your curve ball more often? It's good enough right now to use in clutch situations."

Sandy listened carefully, thought it over for a couple of days, and tested Sherry's advice in his next start. The results were unbelievable. Koufax had discovered the key to his future pitching success.

With his modified fastball and wicked curve flaming past the hitters and into the strike zone, Koufax began to win consistently. That year he picked up 18 wins against 13 losses. He struck out 269 batters—breaking Christy Mathewson's 58-year-old National League record—and gave up just 96 bases on balls.

In 1962 a finger ailment kept Sandy out of action for half of the season. Nevertheless, he managed to win 14 games, including his first no-hitter—a 5–0 triumph against the New York Mets. In 1963 Koufax won 25 games and lost only five. The big game that year was an 8–0 victory over the San Francisco Giants—his second no-hitter. Then, in 1964, his 19-win season was highlighted by still another no-hitter, this time against Philadelphia.

With that third no-hitter, Sandy had tied Bob Feller, Cy Young, and 19th-century pitcher Larry Corcoran for the most lifetime no-hit games. But the best was still to come. On September 9, 1965, Sandy pitched a game that would go down in baseball history as a major league classic.

The Dodgers were playing a home game against the Chicago Cubs. Starting for the Cubs that night was Bob Hendley, a veteran left-hander who relied more on strategy and control than on speed. Through the early innings, both Koufax and Hendley set down every batter who faced them. And after four-and-one-half innings, not one runner had reached first base.

In the bottom of the fifth, the Dodgers scraped together a run without the benefit of a base hit. Outfielder Lou Johnson became the game's first base runner by drawing a walk. He moved over to second

Koufax loses his cap on the way to winning his fourth no-hitter—a perfect game—on September 9, 1965.

on a sacrifice. When Johnson tried to steal third, Chicago catcher Chris Krug overthrew the bag and the Dodger fielder came all the way home on the play. Although Hendley had yet to give up a base hit, he and the Cubs were behind 1–0.

The sixth inning came and went, and still neither pitcher had allowed a single base hit. By then, the fans realized they were watching one of the most exciting pitching duels in major league history. Hendley was still working toward a no-hitter, while Koufax had still not allowed a single runner to reach first base.

Koufax blanked the Cubs one-two-three in the top of the seventh. But in the bottom of the frame Hendley lost his no-hitter when Lou Johnson blooped a double to right. The Chicago southpaw then retired the side with no further trouble, so the score remained 1–0, Dodgers.

As Koufax came out for the eighth, the stadium was charged with tension. But Sandy remained cool enough to strike out Ron Santo, Ernie Banks, and Byron Browne in order. He was now only three outs away from a perfect game.

The Dodgers tried to score an insurance run in the bottom of the inning to give Koufax some breathing room, but they couldn't touch Hendley for another hit. Still, in all the excitement over Koufax's possible perfect game, the 29,139 fans weren't at all impressed with Hendley's brilliant effort.

All the Dodger rooters could think about was Koufax. The crowd rode on every pitch he delivered in the ninth inning. The first man up was catcher Chris Krug, the good-glove, light-hitting catcher of the Cubs. After fouling off a couple of fastballs, Krug finally swung and missed on a 2–2 pitch. One down.

The next Chicago batter was pinch-hitter Joe Amalfitano, an experienced big leaguer. Sandy's first pitch burned into catcher Jeff Torborg's glove for a strike, the second was fouled off, and the third sailed right past Amalfitano for strike three. Two down.

To the plate came Harvey Kuenn, another pinch-hitting veteran. Now only Kuenn stood between Sandy and his perfect game. With all the concentration he could muster, Koufax began his windup. A blazing fastball over the plate: Strike one!

Koufax mopped his brow, leaned in, got his sign from Torborg, and fired. In the process, Sandy's hat fell off, an indication that he was pressing too hard: Ball one!

Once again Koufax wound up. He took a giant stride toward the plate and rocketed another high, fast one: Ball two!

With the count at 2–1, Sandy hurled again. Kuenn swung around quickly and missed the ball completely: Strike two!

An eerie silence settled over the ballpark as Koufax planted his foot against the rubber slab and peered in for his next pitch. Taking a deep breath, he reared back and sent a fastball blazing toward the plate. Kuenn dug in, swung, and missed: Strike three!

Koufax had his perfect game. And with it, he also had the fourth no-hit, no-run game of his career. Sandy Koufax had just become the only pitcher in baseball history to achieve that distinction. Not quite 30 years old, Sandy was just approaching his peak. It seemed only a matter of time before the Dodger ace would rack up still another no-hitter. But time was running out on Koufax. For years, Sandy had been

Sandy is surrounded by his jubilant teammates after his perfect game. The scoreboard shows no runs and no hits for the Cubs.

troubled by a severe case of arthritis in his left elbow. It had gotten so bad that he had to pack ice on his swollen arm after every game, and each appearance was followed by hours of agonizing pain.

Through it all, Koufax finished the 1965 campaign with 26 wins and then went on to pitch the Dodgers to a World Series victory. In 1966 he won 27 games, his highest total of wins ever.

But then, in an emotion-filled press conference, after the Dodgers had lost the 1966 World Series to the Baltimore Orioles, Koufax announced his retirement from baseball. He was only 31 years old, but the twelve-year strain of powerhouse major league pitching had taken its toll on his left arm.

"I'm calling it quits," Sandy sadly declared, "because the doctors tell me I may face the possibility of a serious injury to the arm if I continue any longer. Rather than see the team hurt, or myself, I've decided to bow out while I'm still ahead."

Sandy Koufax was so far ahead that it would take years before any other pitcher would even come close to catching up with his remarkable accomplishments. By 1972, when he became the youngest member ever elected to the Hall of Fame, his perfect fourth no-hitter was still an unattainable goal for baseball's best hurlers.

JOE DiMAGGIO

The Longest Hitting Streak

On the morning of May 15, 1941, a frustrated Joe DiMaggio sat worrying about his batting slump. Over the last 13 games, the Yankee slugger had only nine hits to show for 39 times at bat, and his season's average had shrunk to .306.

Of course, to most major leaguers a .306 batting average would be a welcome worry; but DiMaggio wasn't just any ballplayer. A tall, lean man who carried a big bat, DiMaggio was known as the Yankee Clipper. In his five years with New York, Joe's incredible hitting had made him a natural successor to the throne once occupied by New York Yankee batting kings Babe Ruth and Lou Gehrig.

Joseph Peter DiMaggio was the son of an Italian fisherman. Joseph DiMaggio, Sr., had emigrated to the

United States from Sicily and settled in the bay area of San Francisco. It was there that Joe, Jr., was born on November 25, 1914.

With nine children in the family, the DiMaggios could have formed their own baseball team. As children, Joe, his older brother Vince, and Dom, the youngest DiMaggio, loved the sport. All three signed with the San Francisco Seals, one of the top-rated Triple A teams during the 1930s. Eventually, Vince played for the Pittsburgh Pirates, while Dom played for the Boston Red Sox.

Joe was called up by the Yankees in 1936 and immediately set the American League on fire. In his rookie season he hit .323, socking out 29 home runs. His outstanding play at the plate and in center field helped the Yankees to a World Series victory that year.

Joe batted .346 in 1937 and .324 in '38. In 1938 he was even better, leading the league with a .381 average and winning the Most Valuable Player award.

In 1940 the Yankees lost the pennant for the first time in five years, but Joe D. hit a rousing .352 for his second straight batting crown. So, with a background like that, he had to be disappointed with his .306 "slump" in the early months of '41.

To make matters worse, the Yankees were slumping along with Joe. After losing four straight games in mid-May, the Bronx Bombers found themselves in fourth place with a lackluster 14–14 record. The first-place Cleveland Indians were five and one-half games ahead of New York, and the Yankees seemed unable to narrow the gap.

Yankee pennant chances sunk even further on the gray, cloudy afternoon of May 15. DiMaggio singled once off Chicago White Sox pitcher Edgar Smith. But the Yankee Clipper's single was lost in a barrage of White Sox hits as the Yankees went down in a 13–1 rout. All through the next week Joe kept getting one or two hits a game, and before long he had hit safely in ten games.

Meanwhile, the Yankees continued to lose about as many games as they won. And while Joe was quietly building up his streak, he was having troubles of his own. A strained neck muscle was causing him severe pain, and each big swing only made him feel worse.

With his neck still bothering him, DiMaggio broke loose on May 27 against Washington pitching. Joe went four-for-four and blasted a 415-foot home run into the left-field stands as the Yanks swamped the Senators 10–8. DiMaggio was now on a twelve-game tear.

Two days later a downpour ended a game after only five innings, but a fourth-inning single made it possible for Joe to add the abbreviated game to his growing total. Throughout the month of May, the press paid only mild attention to Joe's streak. But when Di-Maggio hit safely in his 20th straight game on June 3, the sportswriters began turning out story after story on the Yankee star.

By then it was duly noted that the record hitting

streak for a New York Yankee (shared by Earle Combs and Roger Peckinpaugh) was 29 games. Then there was the American League record of 41 held by George Sisler—and the all-time, 44-game mark established by Baltimore's Wee Willie Keeler in 1897.

As Joe's streak lengthened, he found himself more and more in the spotlight. Baseball fans all over the country became obsessed with his progress and followed his every move, both on and off the field. Men, women, and children would gather around their radios in the evening to find out if DiMaggio had hit that day. Everywhere he went, people stopped the outfielder, begging for his autograph. Before long, DiMaggio couldn't even go to a restaurant without being approached by fans, so the shy slugger spent most of his leisure time in his room. As the streak continued, his only social outing was an occasional trip to a local movie house. There, nobody would recognize him in the dark.

As the weather warmed up in June, DiMaggio's neck problem faded away. Now he and his Yankees, still in fourth place, were ready to move. On June 7, the club came into St. Louis for a weekend series with the Browns. That Saturday the Clipper ripped off three singles as the New Yorkers blitzed the Browns 11–7. And on Sunday the Yanks swept a doubleheader, 9–3, and 8–3, with DiMaggio going four-foreight, hitting three homers and driving in seven runs. His streak was now up to 24 games, and the Yankees were moving in on the first-place Indians.

Joe DiMaggio, the Yankee Clipper, slams the ball and adds another game to his hitting streak early in the 1941 season.

Two games later, against the Chicago White Sox, Joe D. made two spectacular catches and threw out a Chicago runner heading for home. But although he outdid himself in the field, he ran into trouble at the plate. In a tight pitchers' battle, Joe went hitless for nine innings. Then with the score knotted at 2–2 in the tenth inning, he came to bat against Thornton Lee, a tough left-hander. When Lee served up a high fastball, the Clipper lashed out and drove it into the stands. That home run gave the Yanks another victory and boosted DiMaggio's streak to 26 straight games.

By June 15, the Yankees were flying along with DiMaggio. The New Yorkers beat the Indians 3–2 that day for their seventh win in a row, and DiMaggio got a third-inning homer to run his string to 28 games.

DiMaggio tied the Yankee record of 29 games on June 16, but he almost broke his streak the following day against Chicago. After going hitless for most of the game, Joe finally slapped a grounder to Chicago shortstop Luke Appling. The ball took a slight hop and bounced off the infielder's shoulder. It looked like a fielding error to many fans, but the official scorer called it a hit. The fluke single embarrassed DiMaggio, but it kept the streak alive at 30 games—a new Yankee record.

With every game, the tension built. The fans put pressure on him, of course, and Joe pressed himself to keep the streak going. "The pressures didn't mean much to me in my fielding," Joe later explained. "I played the outfield like it was just another game. At bat, it built up a little. Naturally, I thought about the streak. How could I avoid thinking about it? I'd be listening to the news and then they'd say, 'Joe got his hit' . . . or something like that."

Fortunately, Joe was used to playing under pressure. In fact, he had already put together a 61-game hitting streak in his early days in the Pacific Coast League. In 1933 the 19-year-old DiMaggio had ripped the minor league apart while staying calm under mountains of newspaper publicity. The memory of that early streak helped keep Joe cool during his big league run.

On June 20, he rapped Detroit pitching for four hits and helped New York to a 14–4 win. That game ran his hitting rampage to 33 games and raised his season's batting average to .354.

On he went, leading his team up in the standings as the streak built to 37 games. On June 26, however, Joe had another close call in a home game against the Browns. When the Yanks came up in the bottom of the eighth inning, DiMaggio still hadn't gotten his hit. New York was ahead 3–1, and Joe was due up fourth. Unless one of the first three batters got on base or the Browns bounced back in the top of the ninth, he wouldn't get another chance at the plate. A groan went up from the stands as leadoff batter Johnny Sturm popped out. But Red Rolfe brought the fans to their feet by waiting out a walk. Then Tommy Henrich laid down a perfect bunt, sending Rolfe to second—and bringing DiMaggio to the batter's box.

The determined Yankee Clipper dug in against

Eldon Auker, a right-hander with a wicked underhand motion. Auker submarined his pitch in, and Joe slashed it far into left field. The fans let out a gigantic roar, the Yankee players slammed their bats on the dugout roof, and DiMaggio pulled up at second base with his streak intact at 38 games.

As June came to an end, the Yankees passed Cleveland to head the American League standings. Meanwhile, Joe was getting ready to pass George Sisler's American League 41-game mark. On June 27, Joe stretched his streak to 40, and two days later he made his bid for the record. The Yankees were playing a doubleheader in Washington, and 31,000 fans came out to see if the great Joe D. could make it safely through games 41 and 42.

Dutch Leonard started for the Senators in the opener and retired DiMaggio in his first two trips to the plate. But on the third go-round Leonard made the mistake of trying to slip a fastball by the Yankee slugger. DiMaggio lined it into left center for a two-base hit. The streak was now 41 games, equal to Sisler's American League mark.

But between games of the doubleheader, disaster hit. Someone sneaked into the Yankee dugout and made off with DiMaggio's bat. Joe had used the same dark-colored bat all year, and its loss bothered him deeply.

"You'd be surprised how a bat you've been using a long time fits in the hand like a glove," Joe explained. "You can tell if there's a one-ounce difference."

Reluctantly, he lugged Tommy Henrich's club up to the plate in the second game. It may have taken him awhile to get used to the new bat, but he still managed to line a single to left in the seventh inning. That hit gave him sole possession of the American League mark. Now he had only one more record to shoot for: Wee Willie Keeler's standard of 44 games.

Beating Sisler's record took some of the pressure off DiMaggio. "Sure I feel great," he said. "Why shouldn't I? That's one record I've wanted to crack ever since I came up to the major leagues. Now I'm going after that 44-game mark, and I'll keep swinging and hitting as long as I can."

In a doubleheader against the Boston Red Sox in Yankee Stadium on July 1, DiMaggio finally caught up with Keeler. Starting the day with his string at 42 games, the Clipper collected a hit in each contest to tie the legendary Keeler for the all-time record.

After the game, the relaxed and happy Yankee talked about the last tense weeks of the streak. "When I got up around 30 straight games," he said, "I was almost indifferent about it. But when I got up to 35 games, I really got interested in it. I said to myself, just like the human fly when he got up to the 35th floor of the Empire State Building, 'Why not go further?' And that's when I started bearing down."

On July 2, Joe batted safely in his 45th straight game to pass Keeler's record. The big hit came against the Red Sox—a sizzling liner that rocketed over left fielder Ted Williams' head and into the stands for a

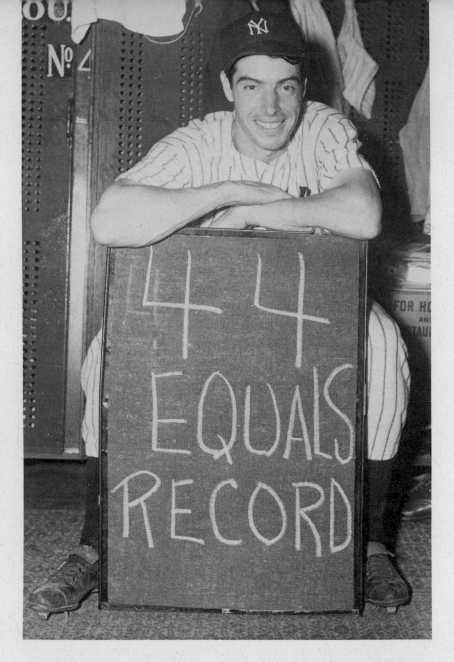

Joe's sign—and his big smile—tell the story after DiMaggio tied Wee Willie Keeler's major league record.

home run. Joe played the rest of the game in a fog as the Yanks went on to pick up their sixth straight victory and their 20th win in the last 24 games.

With the Yankees breezing along in first place, DiMaggio kept right on hitting. On July 4, he received an Independence Day present when an anonymous fan returned Joe's stolen bat to the Yankee clubhouse.

With his favorite bat in hand, DiMaggio ran the streak higher and higher until it reached 56!

On July 17th the Yanks headed into Cleveland's Municipal Stadium for a night game against the Indians. By now, DiMaggio had become a phenomenal gate attraction, and 67,468 fans were on hand to see him go for number 57.

The starting pitcher for the Indians was Al Smith. In the first inning Joe whistled a low liner over the third-base sack. Indian fielder Ken Keltner snagged it on a short hop and snapped it to first just in time to nip DiMaggio.

In the fourth inning Smith walked the Clipper on a 3–2 pitch. Time was growing short as Joe stepped in for his third turn at bat in the seventh inning. He caught a curve ball on the lean part of the bat and shot a low liner towards third. Again Keltner made a great play on the ball, getting it to first ahead of DiMaggio.

In the eighth inning the Yankees pulled ahead 4–1. With two men on base and one out, up came DiMaggio.

Cleveland manager Roger Peckinpaugh (the former Yankee who had held the team's streak record until

Joe busted it) called in Jim Bagby from the bull pen. Bagby had served up a homer to DiMaggio back on June 15, but now he was determined to put an end to the Clipper's streak.

The count ran to 1–1. Then Bagby zinged a fastball into the strike zone. DiMaggio connected and ripped a hot grounder—right into the hands of Lou Boudreau. In a bang-bang situation, DiMaggio's shot was turned into a double play. The streak was over at 56 games.

Joe slides safely into third after hitting in his 56th straight game.

Amazingly, DiMaggio got a hit the next day and then went on to build a new string of 16 games before being stopped again. At season's end, his statistics included a .356 batting average, 30 home runs, and 125 runs batted in. And the Yankees had fared just as well. From their depressing fourth-place beginning, the Yanks finished first in the league by a full 17 games—thanks mainly to Joe, whose invaluable contribution was rewarded with the Most Valuable Player trophy.

The New Yorkers went on to defeat the Brooklyn Dodgers in the 1941 World Series. But while the Yanks had won world championships before—and would undoubtedly win them again—Joe's 56-game streak remained a unique landmark in baseball history.

WILLIE MAYS

Willie Comes Home

There were 35,000 fans in Shea Stadium when Willie Mays came out of the dugout to be introduced—but it seemed more like a million. A deafening roar followed him to home plate, and the cheers approached near-hysteria when he doffed his blue and orange Met cap and waved to the crowd. It was May 14, 1972, and Mays was about to make his debut as a New York Met. After more than 14 years in San Francisco, Willie Mays had finally come home to New York—the place where it all began.

Dressed in a New York uniform, Mays had played his first major league game there 21 years earlier, in 1951. But his team then had been the Giants, who were playing in the old Polo Grounds in New York City. In 1951 Mays had been a shy, insecure rookie—

Willie Mays makes his debut as a New York Met on May 14, 1973.

barely out of his teens—a country boy from Westfield, Alabama, who had been thrust into the limelight in one of the most dynamic cities in the world.

Willie had just been called up to the New York Giants from the minor league Minneapolis Millers.

Although he had been hitting .477 for the Millers, his first road trip with the Giants turned out to be a disaster. He didn't get a hit in 21 times at bat, and his fielding also left a lot to be desired.

After one particularly frustrating road game, the young rookie had sat on his stool in the Giant locker room and wept openly. Giant manager Leo Durocher approached Willie and put his arm around the young Giant.

As a Giant rookie in 1951, 20-year-old Willie gets some words of advice from manager Leo Durocher.

"Please send me back to Minneapolis," Willie begged his manager. "I'm not good enough to play in the big leagues."

Durocher studied the youngster's face, then said, "Willie, as long as I'm manager of this club, you'll be my center fielder."

Willie may have been thinking of that moment as he looked up into the stands of Shea Stadium some 21 years later. Or perhaps he was remembering a happier moment at the Polo Grounds on May 28, 1951. It was shortly after the disastrous road trip, and Willie had yet to get a hit. The Giants were playing the Boston Braves, and as Mays came up to bat the crowd waited anxiously to see if the young Giant could break out of his slump—and live up to his advance rave notices. Boston's ace hurler, Warren Spahn, sent his pitch to the plate and Willie drove it into the left-field stands for a home run—his first major league hit.

That was just the beginning, and before long Mays had established himself as a true Giant star. There were many more heroic home runs, magnificent catches, incredible throws, and hair-raising stolen bases for Willie in the years that followed. But the thing that really endeared him to the New York fans was his total enthusiasm for the game. Willie so loved baseball that for years he would finish a game at the Polo Grounds and then rush straight to the streets of Harlem, where he'd play stickball with the neighborhood kids until it got too dark to see the ball.

Mays remained a favorite of New York fans until

1958 when he and the Giants moved 3,000 miles to San Francisco's Candlestick Park. And there Willie found a whole new legion of fans. During the next 14 years he was a constant league-leader in one department or another. Singles, extra-base hits, home runs, and stolen bases—Willie got them all in record numbers. In a land of Giants, he was the biggest of them all.

By then it was hard to imagine the Giants without Willie—or Willie without the Giants. Yet early in the '72 season it was rumored that the Giants were thinking about trading him. Giant owner Horace Stoneham had once said that Willie would always be a Giant, no matter what. But times had changed since Stoneham had moved his team from New York to San Francisco. Costs had gone up, while attendance figures had dropped. And Willie's once-modest salary had increased tremendously since the move west. By the late 1960s he was one of the highest-paid athletes in the country. So when Horace Stoneham found himself heavily burdened with financial difficulties in the spring of 1972, he approached Joan Payson, the wealthy owner of the New York Mets. "Would the Mets be interested in Willie Mays?" he asked.

Mrs. Payson had always been one of Willie's biggest fans. She had once owned some stock in the old Giant ball club and had often watched him play in New York. So when Stoneham approached her with the idea, Mrs. Payson jumped at the chance to sign Mays.

After 21 years in the majors, Willie was obviously

nearing the end of his career. But the Mets were sure that he could still contribute much to their club. In fact, the Mets were so eager to bring Willie back to New York that they drew up a very generous, long-term contract that would take care of his financial needs for many years to come.

At first, Willie had mixed feelings about leaving San Francisco. He had played some of his best ball there. But then the memories of his great moments in New York came rushing back. New York had *always* been his adopted city, and now he was ready to go home. So, the deal was made. In return for Mays, the Giants received Met pitcher Charlie Williams and a bundle of cash.

When the news story broke, New Yorkers celebrated the occasion by telling and re-telling stories of Willie's legendary feats at the Polo Grounds. From 1951 through 1957, he had won the hearts and affections of the fans as few athletes ever had. Under the bright summer sun he had streaked around the bases with whoops of pure pleasure, belted out home runs with a dazzling grin on his face, and played each game in the Polo Grounds as if it was a birthday party in his honor.

Now it was May 14, 1972, and Willie Mays was back in New York. "Welcome Home Willie" banners fluttered from the stands as Willie stood and listened to the Met fans' cheers. He was 41 years old, and the advancing years showed in his salt-and-pepper hair, in the lines that creased his once-smooth face, and in the weariness that was beginning to cloud his eyes.

But he was still the one and only Willie Mays. And in a few minutes he would be playing first base for the New York Mets in Shea Stadium. To Willie, it almost seemed that he was 20 years old again. The stage was set. Ironically, Willie would be playing his Met debut against his old teammates—the San Francisco Giants. The Giants had selected Sam McDowell to pitch that Sunday afternoon, and Ray Sadecki was on the mound for New York. A light rain delayed the start of the game briefly, but soon the skies cleared and the Mets took the field. Mays received another ovation, which continued until he reached his position at first base. Even as Sadecki pitched to the first Giant batter, most eyes in the stadium rested on Willie.

Sadecki put down the Giants in the top of the first, and then Mays led off the bottom half for the Mets. With each pitch, the fans voiced a chorus of cheers, encouraging Mays to get a hit. The racket in the stands seemed to fluster McDowell, who walked Willie, then proceeded to load the bases with walks to shortstop Bud Harrelson and outfielder Tommie Agee. Then, right fielder Rusty Staub belted a grand-slam home run high over the left-field fence. The crowd roared again as Willie trotted home to score his first Met run.

With the Mets ahead 4–0, things settled down for a while after that dramatic beginning. In the bottom half of the second, Willie came up again and struck out. Then, in the top of the fifth, the Giants broke loose with four runs of their own to tie the game.

Giant relief pitcher Don Carrithers came out to pitch the bottom of the fifth, and as Mays came to the plate, the familiar cry of LET'S GO METS! rang through the stadium. Willie dug in to meet the enemy pitcher—who wore the same uniform Willie had worn for over 14 years.

On the count of 3–2, Carrithers fired in the payoff pitch and Mays swung with all the power he could muster. The bat made contact solidly, sending the ball on a high arc toward the fence in left field . . . and way beyond. It was Mays' 646th career home run—but his first as a Met. The crowd erupted as if he'd just single-handedly won the World Series. They continued to roar as he gleefully circled the bases and the big scoreboard flashed: New York 5, San Francisco 4.

The fans were still buzzing when Met pitcher Jim McAndrew relieved Sadecki in the top of the sixth. The Met right-hander held the Giants in check for two innings, and in the bottom of the seventh Willie came up for his fourth turn at bat. This time he received a standing ovation from the appreciative crowd.

Then, the fans' cheers turned to boos as Carrithers walked their hero. But Willie got his fans right back up on their feet again when he took off for second. Actually, he had missed a sign and was easily cut down at the bag; but as he dusted off his trousers and trotted sheepishly toward the dugout, the fans cheered anyway. As far as they were concerned, Willie could do no wrong.

McAndrew put in four fine innings of relief work,

In 1973, the 41-year-old Mays crosses the plate with his 646th career home run—his first as a Met.

and the game ended with New York in front 5–4. In the Met locker room after the game, Willie received back-slapping congratulations from his teammates. Later, when the writers and photographers arrived, he was surrounded by newsmen all wanting to know how it felt to be back.

"You know New York," Willie beamed. "When they love you, they love you!"

New York kept loving Willie, but there weren't many great moments left for the aging outfielder. His batting average, which had hovered around the .300 mark throughout his long career, began to plummet. Mays finished the 1972 season with a .250 average and went through '73 with a dismal .211. On the field, things were no better. Mays couldn't run nearly as fast or throw as hard as before, and every day he found it harder and harder to play well.

Finally, just two weeks before the end of the 1973 season, Mays announced his retirement. "Willie Mays Night" was celebrated at Shea Stadium on September 25, and a crowd of more than 50,000 well-wishers showed up to say goodbye to the man who had given so much pleasure to baseball fans all over the country.

Many baseball immortals gathered around home plate to say farewell to Willie. Joe DiMaggio was there, as were Duke Snider, Stan Musial, Ernie Banks, Pee Wee Reese, Bobby Thomson, Monte Irvin, and countless other old teammates and rivals. Also on hand was Horace Stoneham, Willie's Giant boss for so many years.

Deeply moved, Willie listened as his friends and fans paid tribute to his great achievements in 22 years of baseball: 660 career home runs, 3,283 hits, 2,062 runs, 1,903 RBI's, and a lifetime batting average of .302.

When all the speeches were over and all the farewell gifts and mementos presented, a teary-eyed Mays grasped the microphone. His words rang out into the night air, and an eerie silence filled the stadium while

On "Willie Mays Night," September 25, 1973, New York's favorite ballplayer says a sad farewell to his fans and friends.

he spoke. After thanking the fans for all their good wishes, Willie Mays said his own goodbye.

"It is a sad day for me," he said. "I may not look sad, but to hear you cheer me, and not be able to do anything about it . . ."

His voice trailed off for a moment, and then he added, "This is my farewell. I thought I'd never quit, but there always comes a time to get out. It's time to quit when you're 42 and hitting .211. We have these kids who are playing, telling me one thing—Willie, say goodbye to America."

COOKIE LAVAGETTO

The Dodgers' Last Hope

The World Series was first played in 1903, and through the years, it produced many exciting pitching moments. But as late as 1947, no World Series pitcher had ever achieved a no-hitter.

A few pitchers *had* come close. In 1906 Ed Reulbach of the Chicago Cubs pitched a one-hitter against the Chicago White Sox, and Herb Pennock of the New York Yankees hurled seven and one-third hitless innings in the 1927 Series before Pittsburgh's Pie Traynor broke up his bid. In 1939 Monte Pearson of the Yankees also went seven and one-third innings before being stopped, and three years later Red Ruffing, another Yank, lost his no-hitter after seven and two-thirds innings. Most recently, in 1945, Claude Passeau of the Chicago Cubs had pitched a brilliant one-hitter against the Detroit Tigers.

But no one had ever witnessed anything like the scene that was taking place at Ebbets Field in Brooklyn, New York, on October 3, 1947. It was the fourth game of the World Series between the New York Yankees and the Brooklyn Dodgers. The Yankees had already won two games to the Dodgers' one. Now, in the bottom of the ninth inning, the Yankees seemed about to pick up their third Series win. More important, New York's Floyd "Bill" Bevens was only one out away from pitching the first no-hit game in World Series history. Only Dodger pinch-hitter Harry "Cookie" Lavagetto stood between Bevens and a no-hitter.

The Yanks were leading 2–1, and the Dodgers had two men out. If Cookie couldn't get on base, the game would be over—and Bevens would have his no-hitter. The tension in the Brooklyn ball park was extraordinary. As Lavagetto stepped into the batter's box, a high-pitched battle cry rang out from behind third base, from the center-field bleachers, and from every other section of the old Dodger stadium.

"Cook-ie-e-e-e!"

Cookie Lavagetto was a 34-year-old utility third baseman and a Brooklyn favorite of long standing. After 14 years in the majors, he was making what seemed likely to be his last appearance in a Dodger uniform. Lavagetto was planning to retire at the end of the season, and as he took his stance against Bevens he wanted more than anything to go out a winner.

As for Bevens, the 31-year-old Yankee right-hander

The 1947 World Series was Dodger third baseman Cookie Lavagetto's last chance for greatness.

from Hubbard, Oregon, knew this was his chance for baseball immortality—perhaps his last chance. After four seasons with the Bronx Bombers, he had a mediocre 40–36 lifetime record. And in 1947 his dismal 7–13 record with the pennant-winning Yankees was especially conspicuous. Bevens realized that if he couldn't contribute something soon, his days in New York were numbered.

This fourth game of the Series had gotten off to a fast Yankee start. In the first inning the New Yorkers had put one run together on two singles, one error, and a walk. Then, in the top of the fourth, Yankee third baseman Billy Johnson had smashed a triple to center and scored when outfielder Johnny Lindell doubled high off the center-field scoreboard. That put New York ahead 2–0.

The Dodgers got one run back—without the benefit of a hit. Bevens had been extremely wild during the early innings, and in the bottom of the fifth it cost him dearly. First he walked Dodger third baseman Spider Jorgensen, then pitcher Hal Gregg. Next, second baseman Eddie Stanky sacrificed, moving the Dodger runners to second and third. Finally, Jorgensen came home when Pee Wee Reese grounded out to shortstop Phil Rizzuto. So at the end of five innings, the Yankees were in front 2–1, and Bevens was on his way to a no-hitter.

That's the way it stayed until the bottom of the ninth. Going into the final inning, "Wild Bill" Bevens had given up eight walks and one run—coming dangerously close to being pulled off the mound on more than one occasion by Yankee manager Bucky Harris. Still, not one Dodger had gotten a hit off his serves.

As the Dodgers came to bat for the last time in the bottom of the ninth, Bevens needed just three more outs for a historic World Series no-hitter. The 33,443 Ebbets Field fans tensed as the first Brooklyn batter, Bruce Edwards, lifted a long fly to left field. But Yankee outfielder Johnny Lindell caught it neatly with his back pressed against the wall. One out!

Carl Furillo was the next batter, and Bevens issued his ninth walk of the game to the Dodger right fielder. Brooklyn manager Burt Shotton then sent rookie Al Gionfriddo in to run for Furillo.

The next man up was Spider Jorgensen. The Dodger third baseman brought moans from the home team fans by lifting a foul to first baseman George McQuinn. Two out! Needing just one more out for his big no-hitter, Bevens got set to face the next batter.

Hugh Casey, the ace Dodger relief pitcher, was due up next. Casey had come into the ball game in the top of the ninth. With the bases loaded and one man out, he had gotten Tommy Henrich to hit a double-play pitch right back to him on the first serve. But since Casey was a pitcher, not a hitter, Shotton went to his bench again.

Out came Pete Reiser. The count on Pistol Pete went to 2-1. On the next Bevens pitch, the fans began to roar as Gionfriddo broke for second base. Yogi

Berra, the rookie Yankee catcher, straightened up and pegged the ball to second base—high. Gionfriddo kicked up a cloud of dust as he slid head-first under shortstop Phil Rizzuto's tag.

"Safe!" signaled umpire Babe Pinelli. Gionfriddo dusted off his uniform and took a cautious lead off the bag. With the count on Reiser now at 3–1, Yankee manager Bucky Harris held up his hand and called for a time out. Then he instructed Bevens to give Reiser an intentional walk.

A cardinal rule of baseball had been broken by Harris. By ordering the Dodger hitter walked, he had placed the "winning run" on base. That unorthodox maneuver would eventually make the Yankee skipper one of the most second-guessed figures in baseball.

Meanwhile, Burt Shotton had his own strategy to think about. Reiser had been nursing a leg injury through the last half of the season, so the Dodger manager called on fast Eddie Miksis to run for his sore-ankled outfielder.

The next scheduled batter was Eddie Stanky, a right-handed batter with little power, so Shotton made another big move. Throughout the game, Cookie Lavagetto had sat on the bench, unused and eager to get in to the game. Now Shotten decided to let the veteran bat for Stanky.

As the Brooklyn runners danced off first and second bases, Cookie took his stance. Bevens took a deep breath, checked Gionfriddo and Miksis, then took a sign from Berra. Finally, he reared back and fired. Strike one!

In the ninth inning of game four, Yankee right-hander Bill Bevens was only one out away from baseball's first World Series no-hitter.

Bevens threw again—a fastball—slightly high and outside. Lavagetto reached out and caught it on the tip of his bat. There was a moment of absolute silence as all eyes in the stadium followed the ball soaring high and far toward the right-field wall.

Yankee outfielder Tommy Henrich had swung over toward right-center for the right-handed pull hitter. Frantically, he chased the ball, racing toward the foul line as fast as his legs could carry him. But it was too late. As he made a desperate leap for the ball, it hit the wall, some six feet above his outstretched glove. By that time, Gionfriddo was rounding third, on his way home with the tying run.

Henrich tried to take the carom cleanly, but the ball scooted under his legs and rolled back toward the infield. The Yank outfielder finally ran it down. Off-balance, he made a weak and hurried throw to McQuinn at the edge of the infield. The big first baseman whirled around and heaved the ball to the plate. Again, too late. For there was Eddie Miksis, sitting on the plate with a big grin on his face—home free with the winning run. The game was over, but Miksis just sat there, laughing gleefully while the Dodger dugout emptied.

The explosion that followed rocked the ball park. Lavagetto was buried under an avalanche of white uniforms as his teammates rushed to congratulate him. The Dodger fans leaped and cavorted on the infield grass, some shedding tears of happiness, others fighting for a chance to touch their hero—Cookie Lavagetto.

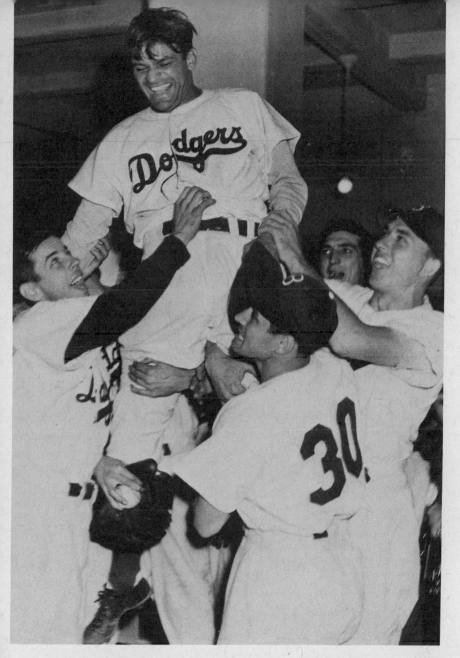

Cookie is lifted to his teammates' shoulders after his ninth-inning double broke up Bevens' no-hitter and won the game for the Dodgers.

Off to the side, Bevens turned away, his head bowed, his glove hanging limply in his left hand. At the very moment that Lavagetto's double banged against the right-field wall, Bevens had seen his whole baseball future slide away from under him. In a daze, he left the mound and disappeared from the joyous scene— noticed by only a handful of observers.

Bevens never again pitched in the major leagues. And even though his last effort was a heart-breaking World Series one-hitter, his name was soon forgotten. But for Cookie Lavagetto, who made only one hit in the entire seven-game classic and then retired as an active player, it was only the beginning. Lavagetto went on to become a big league manager, first with the Washington Senators and then the Minnesota Twins. And even when he left the world of baseball in 1961, he was not forgotten. A hero to millions of fans, he would always be remembered as the batter who broke up a World Series no-hitter at the last possible moment.

CARL HUBBELL

An All-Star Masterpiece

They called him The Stopper, The Meal Ticket, and King Carl. His nicknames held special meaning for all New York Giant fans, and each nickname seemed to fit Carl Hubbell—one of the greatest southpaw pitchers to step on a major league mound.

After a brilliant 16-year career with the Giants, Hubbell was elected to the Hall of Fame. He earned that honor by racking up an amazing list of mound achievements: a total of 253 wins; five straight seasons with 20 or more victories; a National League record for pitching $46\frac{1}{3}$ consecutive scoreless innings; a lifetime earned run average of 2.97; and two Most Valuable Player awards.

And yet, of all the outstanding performances in his legendary career, there is one that stands out above all

135

others. From start to finish it lasted less than one hour, but it will be remembered for as long as baseball is played. The time was July 10, 1934—the place, New York City's Polo Grounds, the site of the second annual All-Star game. It was there that Carl Hubbell, The Stopper, was called on to stop a line-up of the most powerful batters in the major leagues.

Before 48,363 avid fans, the best ball players of both the National and American Leagues squared off for a contest that was billed as The Rematch of Champions. Only a year before, on July 6, 1933, the first All-Star game had been played in Chicago's Comiskey Park, amidst the excitement and pageantry of that city's Century of Progress World's Fair.

Hailed as The Game of the Century, that first All-Star match had pitted the heroes of the National League against the top players in the American League. The American League had come into existence at the turn of the century. But more than 30 years later, the much older National League still thought of its A.L. rivals as upstarts. The newer league was loaded with first-class talent, but its 4–2 victory had been a bitter blow for the Nationals.

But now it was one year later, and the National League was primed to defeat the Americans in their second confrontation. Pitching ace Carl Hubbell got the call to open for the Nationals. His assignment was to stop the big bats of the most awesome collection of batting champions in baseball—a line-up so powerful that nine of its members eventually entered the Hall of Fame.

New York Giant ace Carl Hubbell: the man they called King Carl.

As the game began, the 31-year-old Hubbell strolled purposefully to the mound, looked at the familiar surroundings of the Polo Grounds, and faced his first opponent. Charlie Gehringer, the Detroit Tigers' sensational second baseman, led off the top of the first inning by getting a single off Hubbell.

From within the jam-packed grandstands came a high-pitched yell: "Take the bum out!"

Hubbell heard it, and laughed.

The next man up was Heinie Manush, the slugging Washington Senator outfielder with a sizzling lifetime batting average of .333. With two straight strikes already on him, Manush waited Hubbell out to gain a base on balls.

As Manush threw down his bat and trotted to first base, the whole National League infield converged on Hubbell. First baseman Bill Terry, second baseman Frankie Frisch, shortstop Travis Jackson, and third baseman Pie Traynor all came over to the mound to ask Hubbell if he was all right.

"Sure, fellas," Hub drawled. "Just get back to your positions and don't worry about a thing."

As the hurried conference broke up, a familiar voice pierced the Polo Grounds air. "Take the bum out before it's too late!" yelled the disgruntled fan.

But Hubbell remained cool. He checked the runners, then watched the next man in the line-up, a barrel-chested, pigeon-toed hitter, tap his bat on the plate. It was Yankee immortal Babe Ruth, the most dangerous slugger in the history of baseball. Although he was nearing the end of his great career, the Babe was still an awesome figure. At 6-foot-2 and 215 muscular pounds, he seemed to fill the batter's box. He waved his bat in small circles, as if challenging the very right of Carl Hubbell to even play in the same ballpark with him. The crowd, mostly National League rooters, feared the worst.

Hubbell's fingers tightened around the ball, then released a blazing fastball. Gabby Hartnett, the National League catcher, took the pitch in his glove as the umpire shouted, "Ball one!" Once again, Hubbell's fingers dug into the cowhide. But this time he decided to go with his famous screwball—strike one! Again the screwball—strike two!

The great Babe Ruth had a 1–2 count, and still he hadn't taken the bat off his shoulder. King Carl snaked the next pitch toward the plate—another screwball. Ruth hesitantly cocked his bat, then watched Hubbell's pitch streak by. The screwball caught the edge of the outside corner, and the umpire bellowed, "Strike three!"

Ruth had been completely fooled by the pitch. He was so shocked at the call that he just stood there while the umpire stooped down to dust the plate off for the next batter. Finally, the Babe turned away and slowly headed back to the dugout. Gabby Hartnett's face lit up in a radiant smile as he threw the ball back to Hubbell.

Then, up came Lou Gehrig, the Yankees' Iron Horse. Some 13 years earlier Gehrig had been playing

The awesome American League All-Stars, Jimmy Foxx, Babe Ruth, and Lou Gehrig (left to right): all stopped by The Stopper.

college ball for Columbia University in New York City. After seeing Lou play in one spectacular game, a Yankee scout had raved about the college boy to the club management. "I've just found another Ruth," he shouted.

The Yankees signed Gehrig in 1923, and in the years that followed he more than lived up to their expectations. A league-leading slugger, he added extra fire power to a fierce Yankee line-up that became known as Murderers' Row to rival pitchers all over the league.

But Carl Hubbell refused to be intimidated by the Yankee star. He worked the count on Gehrig to one ball and two strikes and then unleashed another screwball. Gehrig took a ferocious cut—and missed. Strike three! Up jumped the crowd, filling the stadium with roars of delight.

Now it was up to Double X, Philadelphia's super-slugging Jimmy Foxx. In 1933, Foxx had won the American League batting crown with a spectacular .356 average. Only once in his nine major league seasons had his average dipped below the .300 mark— and then it had been .291.

Now with Hubbell's first pitch, the powerful third baseman pulled back his bat and waited for Gehringer and Manush to work a successful double steal. The pitch was a called strike. There were men on second and third, and Hubbell was determined not to let a run score. In quick succession, he turned loose two more screwballs. Helplessly, Foxx flailed at them both.

Strike two! Strike three! King Carl had just retired three of the biggest bats in baseball.

In the bottom of the first, St. Louis' Frankie Frisch hammered out a home run for the Nationals, giving the senior circuit a 1–0 lead over the American League.

In the top of the second, Hubbell went after Al Simmons, Chicago's incomparable center-fielder. Simmons had been the league batting champ twice and had batted over .350 six times in his ten-year career. But now he went down fast, another victim of Hub's dipsy-doodle screwball. The huge crowd was on its feet, bellowing its approval.

Then it was Joe Cronin's turn at bat. Cronin was the playing-manager of the Washington Senators and one of the most reliable clutch-hitters in baseball. But Hubbell was pretty good in the clutch himself. With three smoking screwballs over the heart of the plate, he sent Cronin back to the bench. Incredibly, five of the best major league sluggers had faced Hubbell, and all five had been struck down—and out—by his super-screwball.

The string was finally snapped by Yankee catcher Bill Dickey. With a two-strike count on Dickey, Hubbell got a little careless. He gave the Yank a good inside pitch and Dickey connected for a clean single. The magic spell had been broken. Normalcy returned to the Polo Grounds, and the fans settled back in their seats.

The next man up was the American League pitcher,

Lefty Gomez, another Yankee. While he waited for the first pitch, the cocky southpaw looked down at catcher Gabby Hartnett and whispered, "You are now looking at a man whose batting average is .104. What in the world am I doing up here?"

Not surprisingly, Hubbell got Gomez to strike out, and the side was retired. When the Nationals reached the bench, third baseman Pie Traynor went over to Hubbell and began counting on his fingers. "Ruth, Gehrig, Foxx, Simmons, Cronin!" he marveled. "Hey, Hub, do you put anything on the ball?"

In the third inning Hubbell disposed of Gehringer on a long fly, got Manush out on an easy grounder, walked Ruth, and retired Gehrig on a soft liner to right. In the bottom of the inning, second-baseman Billy Herman was sent in to pinch-hit for Hubbell, and King Carl's incredible pitching performance came to an end.

The nearly 50,000 fans at the Polo Grounds had just witnessed one of baseball's greatest moments, and they weren't ready to see it end so quickly. As Herman took his stance in the batter's box, they began to chant: "We want Hubbell!" However, the chant turned into a happy cheer minutes later when Ducky Medwick hit a three-run homer that boosted the National lead to 4–0.

In the fourth inning the American League battled back furiously with two runs. Then, in the top of the sixth, the big A.L. All-Stars really went to work. Bombarding relievers Lon Warnecke and Van Lingle

The Most Valuable Player in the 1934 All-Star game, Hubble accepts the award from sports columnist Frank Graham.

Mungo with one hit after another, the Americans scored six times to take an 8–4 lead. The Nationals bounced back late in the game with a rally of their own, but eventually lost 9–7.

Ruth and company shared the credit for the American League's victory. But there could be no doubt as to who had been the real hero of the 1934 All-Star game. For three unbelievable innings, Carl Hubbell—The Stopper, The Meal Ticket, the man known as King Carl—had neutralized the most awesome line-up ever assembled in a major league game.

INDEX